A Pilgrimage to the Himalayas

MAHADEVI VARMA

A Pilgrimage
to the Himalayas

AND OTHER SILHOUETTES FROM MEMORY

Translated from the Hindi and with an Introduction by
Radhika Prasad Srivastava and
Lillian Srivastava

PETER OWEN · LONDON

ISBN 0 7206 0164 9

Translated from the Hindi
Smriti ki Rekhyan

UNESCO COLLECTION OF REPRESENTATIVE WORKS
INDIAN SERIES

This book has been accepted in the Indian
Literature Translations Series
of the United Nations Educational, Scientific
and Cultural Organization (UNESCO)

PETER OWEN LIMITED
20 Holland Park Avenue London W11 3QU

First British Commonwealth edition 1975
© 1942, 1975 Mahadevi Varma
English translation © 1975 UNESCO

Printed in England by
Burrup, Mathieson & Co Ltd London

Contents

Author's Preface

The present age's focus on science and rationalism lessens the significance of the emotions because it is feared that they can render men incapable of clear judgement. Despite this trend, man continues to be a mysterious creation equipped with both heart and mind, and has become neither a robot nor a computer. By mere wishing, he cannot experience feelings of joy or sadness, nor become compassionate or cruel. But those emotions which cannot be roused by man's total environment can sometimes be generated by a small element in a significant circumstance. Literature is born out of such moments.

Many facets of this world are so mysterious that they seem incomprehensible and we are unable to rationalize them. Only the emotional side of our nature is able to perceive truths that are beyond logic, and can thus make them decipherable to society. The communication of a society's values comes to us in this way, and literature creates and preserves these values. A writer, although bound by the externals of his environment, is free in his vision of life. That is why the literature of all countries and languages has had the same basic aim. Apart from critical essays, all my writing has sprung from my own sensitive response to what I have seen and therefore my individual creative efforts have been transmutable into a reality which embraces humankind.

During my life's journey, the incidents and individuals that influenced me have become a part of my emotional world. From time to time, in order to relive these emotions, I have written my sketches. It is beyond human capacity to bring back incidents from the past, but it is possible to rejuvenate the deep emotions generated by these incidents. Literature and the arts are like festivals of emotion for the human heart, and by participating in

[7]

these a person is able to shed sadness and lethargy.

My memoirs are not meant to be mere detached descriptions of incidents, nor reportage of my own life story or the life stories of others. Rather, they are emotional journeys begun with the purpose of recreating those moments in which I shared and lived the feelings and experiences of others. When we are able thus to restructure in our minds the happiness or sadness of others, we can widen our emotional horizons and gain a clearer and more expanded life view.

The characters found in my memoirs are outwardly simple people and helpless creatures, but on a deeper level they can be seen as symbols of eternal and primordial truths. I am glad to have had the good fortune to know them. They are not playthings to be displayed by a magician in an auditorium. Observing life, I am reminded of the saying from the epic *Mahabharata*, 'Nothing is greater than man.'

The work of a translator is more difficult than the work of the writer himself, for he has the task of transmuting the living images of one language into those of another. Every language reflects a society's mind and heart throughout its history. That is why attempting to put the ideas of one language into another is like attempting to transplant the fragrance of one flower on to another. The translators of this volume, Lillian and Radhika Prasad Srivastava, have worked with great devotion. I am happy that they have been so successful in the difficult task of getting into someone else's mind and heart.

MAHADEVI VARMA

Introduction

Sartre, while discussing existential psychoanalysis in *L'Etre et le Néant*, puts forward the view that it is some time between the ages of seven and ten that a child decides on the kind of person he is going to be when he grows up. Born 24 March, 1907, Mahadevi Varma was only nine years old when her grandfather, whose word was law to her parents, decided that it was time she was officially married. According to age-old traditions she was, of course, not consulted in the matter. When the new father-in-law was told by the Brahmin priest that the stars would not be favourable for the subsequent consummation visit of the bride until a few more years had passed, he insisted that she be sent to her husband immediately for at least a week. Wishing her well, the grandfather thereupon dispatched the crying girl to the small town for a week's stay.

Mahadevi remained there for only one day. She is reported to have done nothing but weep from the moment she arrived, refusing all food. Next morning she began vomiting and the father-in-law, a man steeped in the old traditions, reluctantly allowed her to be sent home.

It seems as though at that point she indeed made her choice of what she would be when she became an adult — a rebel and a champion of women's rights. She was later to uphold these in her essays on the condition of women in India. As a woman, she experienced a conflict between the feminine traits demanded by society and partly intuitive, and the anger roused in her by the subordinate and demeaning position of women in that society. This conflict may have led to her characteristic restlessness as

[9]

she matured. As a writer, the emotional response predominates in
her poetry, the intellectual in her prose.

A follower of the Arya Samaj movement, her father was a
believer in the predominance of reason in life; her mother, a devotee
of idol worship and of the hymns of the saint poetess Mirabai
and the poets Tulsidas and Sur, was ruled more by her emotions.
Here again was a division, with one parent appealing to Mahadevi's
mind, the other to her heart.

When she received her BA degree in 1929, her husband's
family asked that she be returned to their fold to live the life of
an orthodox daughter-in-law. But Mahadevi firmly declined. Mis-
understanding, her father thought that his beloved daughter, who
had a mind of her own, wished to marry someone else of her own
choice. Casting convention aside, he wrote to Mahadevi that he
would be willing to convert the family to another religion which
would allow divorce so that she could marry again. However, she
replied that she would neither go back to the husband who had
been selected in her childhood, nor marry anyone else. She kept
her word and still lives alone in the university town of Allahabad
in North India, surrounded by her pets – dogs, cats, rabbits and
peacocks – and an assortment of human characters who have
attached themselves to her household over the years.

By the time she had obtained her BA degree, she had already
begun to achieve some recognition in the sphere of Hindi literature,
but the world seemed very gloomy to the young Mahadevi, as she
observed the prevailing moral and social degradation of women in
the early decades of twentieth-century India. Women were regarded,
and treated, as unlettered playthings and servants for men. Overwhelmed by sadness, she decided to become a Buddhist nun.
However, on going to the Himalayas to be ordained by a Ceylanese
priest, she found that he would only talk to her while hiding behind
a wooden shield, lest any unsubjugated sexual passion might distract
him. Mahadevi was thoroughly disillusioned; she felt it impossible
to be ordained by someone who could not even look at her.
She left the mountains and went back to continue her studies,
obtaining an MA in Sanskrit in 1932. She was offered a post at the
University of Allahabad, but declined it and instead became the
head of a new women's college based on the nationalistic ideals of
Gandhi.

Mahadevi's first volume of poetry, *Nihar*, was published in 1930 and was followed by *Sandhya Geet, Dipshika, Saptparna* and others, besides several volumes of memoirs and essays on the condition of women in India and on literature. All her books have gone into several editions and *Smriti ki Rekhyan*, which is here translated, is currently in its twelfth edition. She is considered the foremost modern poet in India and unequalled by any other Hindi prose writer. In 1956 the government of India conferred on her the title of 'Padma Bhushan' in recognition of her status as a distinguished citizen, and the state government of Uttar Pradesh is now in the process of preparing a film on her life and work.

Hindi, a language spoken by more than two hundred million people in India, has several dialects; many of these have their own literature. One dialect, Brij, was the favourite of the poets, but at the beginning of this century Brij was discarded and the dialect in which only prose had previously been written was adopted for poetry also. This is now standard usage in Hindi literature and is used by Mahadevi in both her poetry and prose. While she is able to write and converse fluently in English, she has not written in that language, nor has she translated any of her works, since during the struggle for Independence, she vowed to Mahatma Gandhi, for reasons of national pride, not to use English.

When Mahadevi began writing, Hindi poetry had begun to take on new life. A generation of poets who had been exposed to English poetry had emerged and were shifting the emphasis from poetry as a vehicle of ideas to its function as a generator of images. Mahadevi is considered to be one of the foremost representatives of this group and in her hands the formerly stilted poetic tradition began to vibrate with new images and feelings, a new symbolism. The poets of her age claimed to be the creators of a mystical poetry which reinforced monism by means of images charged with anguish and pathos. In the poetry of Mahadevi we find the pinings and frustrations of a woman expressed in the poignant universal images of sky, dawn, evening, earthen lamps, rivers, and so on. She is considered to have written the best lyrics of modern India.

In her prose she deals generally with the disinherited poor people of India, chained by tradition, ignorance and heartrending poverty. Her two most famous books, *Smriti ki Rekhyan* and *Atit ke*

Chalchitra, an earlier book which has not yet been translated, are classics of modern Indian prose. They describe India as it was in the 1930s and 1940s before the country gained its independence. No one else has written so acutely and graphically or spun such pathetic yet somehow humorous stories of the common people of the period. In the process she gives us insights into their modes of thought and behaviour, their social norms and religious beliefs, all of which were in the process of breaking up or being redefined, but were still pursued by simple folk who yet firmly believed in the truth and eternity of the old ways.

Smriti ki Rekhyan comprises seven 'episodes'. A curious combination of memoirs, essays and sketches, they have the flow and gripping interest of stories. Mahadevi's tendency to add her own comments and evaluations to the incidents does not normally obstruct the flow of the stories; they serve as poetic asides.

In the process of translation we have assumed that the reader is generally unfamiliar with details of Indian life and also with Hindi terms, and have therefore endeavoured to clarify within the text as many of these terms as possible without distorting the author's style. Those terms which have no clear or uncumbersome English equivalent are further defined in the Glossary. Since Hindi is written in the Devnagari script, transliterations of terms into English spelling are open to variation; those spellings have been used which seemed most closely to provide the reader with an idea of the sound intended in the original.

We wish to acknowledge the kind co-operation and valuable assistance of Daniel L. Milton and the UNESCO Department of Culture in preparing this manuscript.

LILLIAN SRIVASTAVA
RADHIKA PRASAD SRIVASTAVA

Bhaktin

Looking back now, it seems to me as though an aeon has passed since tiny, emaciated Bhaktin came to me, thin lips pursed and small eyes hiding deep wisdom. But when anyone asks her how long we have been together, she half closes her eyes as if deep in thought and, tilting her chin a bit upward, says confidently, 'Yes – I've been with this lady for fifty years – maybe even longer.' It seems as though Bhaktin doesn't realize that by these calculations I would be at least seventy-five years old and she herself would long since have passed the century mark. Even if she were aware of this, I doubt that she would reduce the span of time which measures the length of her companionship with me. It is much more likely that a few years from now she will stretch the period to one hundred years, ignoring the burdensome age of one hundred and fifty which I shall be forced to carry with me.

Bhaktin, the daughter of a cowherd, serves me in as eager and devoted a way as Hanuman, the monkey god, served Lord Rama. Her real name is Lakshmi, like the goddess of wealth, but just as the implications of my name Mahadevi, great goddess, are beyond my reach, so the wealth of the goddess Lakshmi could not possibly be inscribed in the curved fate lines of her palm. While many people go through life carrying an inappropriate name, Bhaktin in her shrewdness does not disclose the misnomer. When she first came to me looking for a job she did disclose her true name, along with other details of her life, in order to give an honest introduction to herself, but she particularly asked me not to call her this. If I myself had been able to think of a good pseudonym to use in my writing I would have done so – but how could I explain this to a simple village woman? Seeing the string of prayer beads around her neck I renamed her Bhaktin, the pious one, and she seemed deeply moved by her new name.

Even a partial understanding of the idiosyncrasies of Bhaktin's character would be impossible without knowing the brief story of her life. She was the only daughter of a pugnacious cowherd from the historic village of Jhusi, near Allahabad, and she had been brought up under the proverbial malevolence of a stepmother. When she was five, she was married to the youngest son of a prosperous cowherd family from the neighbouring village of Hadia. By marrying off his daughter at this early age her father earned the distinction of being two steps ahead of the laws prescribed in the sacred Shastras: first, she was properly married before the enjoined age of seven, and then, when a few years later nine-year-old Bhaktin was sent to her husband's home, the father acquired the virtue of a creditor who returns someone else's property without being asked to do so.

Being jealous of her husband's deep love for his daughter, the stepmother was vigilant in protecting her husband's property for herself, and so she did not let Bhaktin know when her father fell fatally ill, sending information only when he was already dead. Bhaktin's mother-in-law, too, in order to avoid hearing Bhaktin wail, did not say anything except that since Bhaktin had not been to her father's house for a while it was time to go for a visit. Dressed in a new sari and jewellery, the girl was sent off, the unexpected kindness giving wings to her feet. However, when she reached the outskirts of the village she slowed her steps, for from all sides she heard softly whispered, 'Ah, how late Lakshmi has arrived.' Pushed forward by the strangely sympathetic glances of the village women, she went on to her old house. Once there, she found no sign of her father, and her stepmother's outbursts contained no welcome for her. Badly shaken and inwardly fuming at her stepmother's insults, she turned back to her husband's place without even drinking a sip of water from her father's house. Furious with her stepmother, she turned in anger to her mother-in-law and ripping the jewellery from her body she threw it at her husband to express her feeling of irreparable loss at the death of her father.

In the second chapter of her life, too, sadness far outweighed happiness. One after the other she gave birth to three brown and round-faced daughters, and her mother-in-law and sisters-in-law did not hesitate to show in their faces their disdain for her performance. After all, the mother-in-law had managed to produce three sons, all potential wage earners, and by doing so had earned the right to rule the household and to be respectfully called 'the ancestress'. Bhaktin's two elder sisters-in-law were candidates for the same privilege by virtue of their having given birth to a succession of ugly sons. Having digressed from the family tradition of producing sons, the youngest daughter-in-law was bound to be penalized.

While the two elder sisters-in-law sat and gossipped, and their ugly sons wallowed in the mud, Bhaktin would churn, pound, grind and knead, and her tender daughters would collect cow-dung and make cakes of it to be dried for fuel. At meal times, the elder sisters-in-law would feast on fine white sugar and thick boiled milk poured over rice, and would give the cream from the boiled milk to their sons. Bhaktin, on the other hand, would get only a lump of coarse brown sugar and some whey in a wooden pot, while her daughters received only cheap fried lentils and corn.

Fortunately, in the established social hierarchy, there was no way of separating the husband from the wife, whose qualities gleamed like a polished gem. All the taunts and complaints of his family only made him love her more. The sisters-in-law, in line with prevailing custom, were beaten black and blue by their husbands on the smallest pretext, but Bhaktin was never once struck by her husband. He seemed to comprehend instinctively that his wife was the big-hearted daughter of a brave man. And in truth he must have been extremely fond of his hardworking, bright and loyal wife, for how else could she have succeeded in separating him from his brothers and setting up an independent household. Since she was the only one who did any work on the land, she knew the exact value of each cow, bullock, field and grove. By outwardly pretending dissatisfaction with her husband's share when the land was partitioned, she managed to secure the best fields, cows, bullocks and groves and as time passed, the couple's hard work helped turn the land to gold.

One day, after marrying his eldest daughter with great fanfare, Bhaktin's husband died. Bhaktin, at twenty-nine, was left with two small daughters still playing in the mud and the care of a struggling

household. He could not have been more than thirty-six years old
when he died, but Bhaktin now refers to him as the 'old man'. She
argues that since she has grown old, her husband in heaven must
also have aged, and not to call him an old man would be an insult
to him.

Predictably, seeing Bhaktin's ripening green fields, her fat cows
and she-buffaloes, and the fruit-laden trees, the mouths of her
sisters-in-law began to water. They knew that the only way to get
back this prospering land was to persuade Bhaktin to marry again.
But Bhaktin, wise since childhood, did not fall into their trap.
Angered at their suggestions and stamping her feet until the courtyard shook, she shouted, 'I'm not a cat or a dog. If the day ever
comes that I like a man, then maybe I will leave here. Otherwise
I'll stay on and make you as jealous as I can. You'd better listen
to what I'm saying.'

She did not agree to give away even a thimbleful of the fields
acquired by her father-in-law, her husband's grandfather, and their
ancestors before them. On the contrary, taking advice from a guru,
she adorned herself with a string of beads, shaved off her oiled hair
in memory of her husband and proclaimed her resolve to remain a
widow and continue living in the village. To protect her property in
the future, she married off her youngest daughters and asked her
oldest son-in-law, who had been selected by her late husband, to
live with her. That is where the third chapter of her life began.

Bad luck still seemed determined to waylay her. Bhaktin's eldest
daughter became a widow as she stepped from adolescence into
womanhood. This tragedy brought a ray of hope to the elder
brothers-in-law and their good-for-nothing but determined sons.
The eldest nephew brought home his wife's brother, whose sole
interest was in partridge fighting, to marry the widowed cousin, well
aware that if the marriage occurred all the property would again
be under their control. But the daughter of Bhaktin was no less wise
than her mother; she refused to accept him and this pre-arranged
match. Bringing in an outsider would not suit the purposes of the
cousins, so the marriage suggestion was left hanging. Nevertheless,
while the mother and daughter tilled their fields with great devotion,
the supporters of the rejected potential bridegroom schemed
together to force him on the widowed daughter.

One day while Bhaktin was away the unwanted bridegroom

forcibly entered the daughter's room and latched the door from inside. In the meantime, his supporters began collecting villagers in front of the house. After thrashing the intruder, the brave young woman opened her door and found a ready-made audience standing in front of the house. The village elders were puzzled as to what to do about the situation. On the one hand, the partridge-fighting expert insisted that he had gone inside by invitation; on the other, the daughter pointed to the print of her hand on his cheek as proof of her affront. The assembly of elders met to separate the wheat from the chaff, and, gravely nodding their heads, they agreed that Kalyug, the immoral age through which they were passing, accounted for the trouble. Delivering a judgement with no possibility of appeal, they opined that while either of the parties might be right or both might be telling untruths, since they had both come out of the same closed room they must now live together as husband and wife; only in this way would the evil of Kalyug be expiated. The affronted daughter bit her lip in desperation until blood oozed out, while the future mother-in-law looked at the unwanted bridegroom with daggers in her eyes. The marriage relationship did not prove a happy one, for the son-in-law, now absolved from worldly worries, spent all his time in partridge fights; the daughter meanwhile burned with impotent rage.

The cows, bullocks and fields, once tended with great care, now languished under the pressures of family squabbles. It soon became difficult to scrape up enough money to pay the annual rent. Where had happiness gone? The landlord, who had not received his rent, forced Bhaktin to stand out in the sun for a whole day. This insult was the greatest blow to her pride, and the next day she left for the nearby city in search of a way to earn her bread.

With her clean-shaven head covered by the edge of a coarse, dirty sari, and one ear peeping out as if alert to every sound, Bhaktin's fourth, and perhaps last, chapter of life began in my domestic service, and its complete import is yet to be fathomed.

Noting in her dress a curious mixture of domesticity and renunciation, I queried doubtfully, 'Are you sure you know how to cook?' Twisting her upper lip and pouting slightly with her lower lip, she answered with assurance, 'What's so hard about cooking? I can make chappatis, boil lentils and fry vegetables. What more could you want?'

Early the next morning, pouring a few glasses of water over her head and sprinkling water on the clean sari I had given her, in order to purify it, she paid homage to the rising sun in the still dark eastern sky and to the holy peepal tree sprouting in the eastern courtyard by pouring two glasses of water on the ground. Closing her nostrils with two fingers of one hand she meditated for two minutes, then drew a line with charcoal around the kitchen area, thus proclaiming the boundaries of her empire. It now began to be clear to me that our relationship would not be a smooth one.

Normally I am not particularly concerned about my meals, but in my family I am known for my culinary art, and one expert is bound to criticize another. However, sensing unspoken prohibition in Bhaktin's suspicious looks, and knowing the depth of feeling of believers in untouchability concerning their meals, their tantrums and willingness to go hungry rather than accept meals touched by someone else, the black charcoal line became inviolable, and I decided to respect it. Helpless, lying on my bed with an open book resting on my nose, I tried to push out of my mind the picture of the unauthorized person puttering in my kitchen.

At mealtime, when I took my seat outside the charcoal line, she laid a plate in front of me and, face beaming with self-satisfaction and happiness, began to serve the food – four chappatis, dark, charred and four times thicker than they should be, and thick lentil curry. I quickly threw a wet blanket on her enthusiasm as I said, on the verge of tears, 'What is this mess you have cooked?' She appeared stunned.

'Well – the chappatis did get a little burned while I was trying to bake them better, but they are all right. There were some vegetables available, but as long as I was making lentils, what was the need for vegetables? This evening I'll make vegetables and not lentils. And then, you don't like either milk or ghee, otherwise I would have made something out of them.'

She offered to grind a chutney of tamarind and red chillies, and if I couldn't manage with this, she would give me a lump of jaggery which was still tied in the bundle brought by her from the village. What else did city people eat? Besides, she was not boorish or incompetent. Her father-in-law, his father, the mother-in-law of her mother-in-law and so on, had given many verbal certificates as to her expertise in cooking.

Following her pregnant lecture, not liking jaggery and lacking appetite for ghee, I ate one dry chappati with a dab of lentil curry. Despite the meal, I was cheerful when I reached the university, and while reading logic I brooded over the contrasts between city and village life.

I had made arrangements for a separate cook in order to help me improve my health and to mollify the worries of my relatives, but as it turned out there was no question of special meals prepared just for me. This old peasant woman had so awakened me to life's simplicities that I began to ignore my inconveniences, and, after that, how could there be any search for luxuries? Besides, while it had become second nature to Bhaktin to try to mould others according to her own wishes, she could not even imagine any change in her own character. That is why I have become more of a villager now, whereas she is still totally immune from urban influences. Millet stew cooked at night tastes good with whey in the morning; pua made with corn and studded with sesame seeds is less appetizing when it's hot; kichri of fried corn and green corn is tasty; halvah made from white mahua is the best in the world. These dishes are turned out for me by Bhaktin, but even the most common sweets of the city have never entered her toothless mouth.

Despite my day-in and day-out annoyance with her, she has not learned to wear a clean sari. On the contrary, she will mess up my own clean saris under the guise of pleating them. She has helped me remember many folk stories prevalent in her dialect, but on being summoned she still responds in the casual village way, and has not learned the respectful form of address characteristic of the city.

It would be difficult to say that Bhaktin is the epitome of goodness, for she is certainly not free from frailties. She does not have the honesty of the mythical king, Harish Chandra, but neither is she comfortable in her evasions of truth. The solution to the mystery of how my loose change, left here and there, gets into a tin container is known to her, but if this is even casually pointed out Bhaktin issues an invitation to a series of arguments in which even a top logician would be defeated. This is her own house, so she carefully squirrels away the money left here and there; is that theft? Her greatest ambition is to keep me happy, so what harm is there in slightly twisting words in order to avoid putting me in bad humour? Even Dharamraj, the master of heaven, must do this much thieving and lying, for how else could he continue to please the Almighty God?

Questions of interpretation of the laws in the sacred Shastras are also resolved by Bhaktin according to her convenience. I do not like to see women shave off their hair, so I prohibited her from doing so. Nonchalantly she responded, 'But it's written in the Shastras.' Out of curiosity I asked what was written in the Shastras. She promptly shot back the answer, 'If you go on a pilgrimage and get your head shaved, you get salvation.' To which particular Shastra this curious saying is attributed I could not determine; defeated, I kept quiet and now every Tuesday* her head gets shaved by a poor barber whose razor has been duly washed in the holy water of the river Ganges.

But it would be wrong to say that she is stupid or does not understand the power of learning and mind. She takes great pride in my reading and writing, and through this she fulfils her own need of education. When I once ordered that each employee in my college must sign his name on his pay cheque, this created a problem for her. She did not want to undergo the torment of learning how to write; besides, it would be below her dignity to sit in the same class with women bullock-cart drivers. This would be an insult to her age. She began murmuring to herself, 'My mistress is busy all the time reading or writing. If I started to do this, too, then who would look after the house?' The others were so impressed by her logic that she thereupon took it on herself to assume the role of school inspector and began checking the classes, commenting on the alphabet writing of one, the slow-moving hand of another and the slow mental processes of still others. In the end, since she was my personal employee, she was not required to sign for her pay, and so without any education she had become a guru.

She is an expert not only in finding proof for her reasons, but also proof for her lack of reason. To improve her own status, for instance, she would like others to believe her mistress is unique. But for this she needs evidence. Once I was extremely busy, both with my painting and with examining answer books. She bustled around admonishing those within hearing distance: 'Poor thing. She is busy working all the time and you lot don't lift a finger.

*Tuesday is a holy day.

Come on, let's help her out.' Everyone knew that no help could be rendered in such work and, admitting their inability to be of assistance, they would escape from Bhaktin. Having this clear proof that no one was capable of sharing my work, she began wildly exaggerating my importance – no one knew how to work like her mistress; that is why no one dared to come in and help her.

To admit that even she could not help me would have been an admission of inferiority, so she would sit on the doorstep of my study and repeatedly ask for work. Tying answer books together, placing an incomplete canvas in the corner, washing the colour palette and sometimes wiping the mat with the edge of her sari signified to her eyes her own superior intelligence. While the others would not even dare to imagine helping her mistress, she was able to do many things. Similarly, when a book of mine is published her face beams with happiness like the hidden light flooding from a bulb as its switch is turned on. When alone, she touches the book repeatedly and, drawing it near her eyes, turns it in her hands as if searching for evidence of her share of help. The self-satisfied look in her eyes shows she is not disappointed in her search. But this is natural.

When I am trying to finish a painting and will not leave my easel for meals despite her repeated requests, she brings me butter-milk or a cup of tea made of tulsi leaves so that I do not go hungry. After the day's work, when the lights of the college dormitory have all been extinguished and I begin to work on completing an article or composing a poem, the doe, Sona, seated near the settee, stops ruminating; the dog, Basant, seated on his bed, closes his eyes and hides his mouth in his small paws, and the cat, Godhuli, snuggles into my pillow and goes to sleep. But in order not to leave me alone in the stillness of the night, Bhaktin sits on a mat in the corner and, squinting her eyes because of the glare of the electric light, patiently remains awake. She does not even doze, for the moment I raise my eyes her dim eyes follow my glance. If I look at the bookrack behind my bed, she gets up and asks the colour of the book I want; if I drop my pen, she brings the inkpot; and when I put aside the papers in front of me, she begins shuffling the other files.

Although I go to sleep late, I get up early, but Bhaktin has to rise even earlier, for Sona is eager to be outside frisking about, Basant wants the door opened and Godhuli takes the chirping of the birds as an invitation to go preying.

Bhaktin has been my lone companion in all my wanderings. Just as she insists on walking a few steps ahead of me to face the dangers on the narrow, undulating footpaths to the Himalayan temples of Badrinath and Kedarnath, so also she never forgets to be just behind me on the dusty footpaths of the village. Any time, under any conditions, whenever I am required to go out, I find Bhaktin trailing behind me.

Seeing the Second World War encroaching on the borders of India, people became apprehensive, and Bhaktin's daughter and son-in-law came to take her away to the safety of the village. But she would not go despite their persuasion, for this would mean leaving me and she is not willing to do this until her last day.

When the continuing war created further panic and people chose to run away rather than face it, Bhaktin stood before me for the first time with the traditional humility of a servant, and begged me to come to her village. She offered to keep my clothes on the box used for storing fuel, promising to spread her new sari over it first; she would build a makeshift bookrack by pounding nails into the wall and placing wooden planks on them; she would make a soft bed for me by spreading her blanket on stacks of paddy; she would keep my paints and ink in new earthen pots, and my papers would be safely kept in a pot hung from the ceiling.

'I cannot go there – I have no money to live with,' I said, in order to put a stop to her proposal. But the outcome surprised me. Coming close as if she were going to divulge a great secret, she brought her toothless mouth near my ear and softly told me that she had hidden in the ground five times twenty rupees, plus five rupees, and with this sum she could manage everything. The war could not last for ever, and when everything was straightened out we could return to the city again. Bhaktin's miserliness had by this time assumed mountainous proportions, but this one act of benevolence was enough to shatter its core. Such a small sum has no value, but her love for money was widely known and her wish to give it to me was of great significance.

To describe our relationship as that of master and servant would not be accurate, for there can hardly be a master who could not dismiss his employee even if he wished to do so and I have not yet heard of any servant who on being told to leave would disregard the order with a disdainful look. To call Bhaktin a servant would be as inappropriate as claiming for my servants the eternal round of light and darkness, the roses blooming in the courtyard or the mangoes on the trees. They each have their separate existence, and only give us pain or pleasure. Similarly, Bhaktin has her own independent personality, and to delineate its boundaries she has shared my life.

A ray of love and sympathy continually emanates from the contrasting personality traits developed through family troubles and adverse circumstances; that is why those who come in touch with her find natural empathy. Invariably, girls from the college dormitory are to be found in my kitchen getting their milk warmed or tea brewed, or tasting and commenting on my breakfast as they stand on the doorstep. When they see me they fly away like birds, and resume their places only when I withdraw. Making a compromise with the traditional rules of meal untouchability, Bhaktin cooks all her own meals in the morning and hides them in the attic, lest the girls be prevented from coming to the kitchen. Then when she eats she cleans a corner of the kitchen for her own use.

Bhaktin is very familiar with my acquaintances and literary friends, and the degree of her own respect and friendly feelings toward them exactly mirrors my own true feelings. Her intuitive grasp of my inner thoughts amazes me.

Some friends she remembers by peculiarities of physiognomy and dress, some by names mutilated by her. She has increased her knowledge of poetry and poets, but not her respect for them. Seeing the long hair and dishevelled dress of one she would blurt out, 'What? You mean *he* knows how to write poetry?', and immediately her disdain would be obvious. 'He'll never amount to much – he'll do nothing but roam the streets singing and playing.'

Everyone's sorrow touches her. When someone from amongst the students is jailed for participating in the freedom struggle, Bhaktin irritates everyone during the day with her wailing, 'Annihilation is coming, Kalyug is already here, otherwise why would they put little children in jail?' Her sympathy is equally great for jail-going Mahatma Gandhi and for the ordinary freedom fighter.

Because of her upbringing she is as afraid of jail as she is of the world of death. When she sees the high walls of a jail she almost faints. This weakness of hers is now notorious and people tease her by telling her of the possibility of my being put behind bars. It would be wrong to say she is not afraid, but stronger yet is her need to stay with me. Quietly she will ask me how many saris she should wash so that I may not be ashamed on her account, and what things she should pack so that I am not inconvenienced. My assurance that no one can accompany another on such a journey has no meaning for her. She feels more insulted at the prospect of not coming with me than pleased at the thought that I may not have to go. Wherever the master is, the servant will also be. It may be an injustice to lock up the master but it is a horrifying injustice to let the servant go free. If ever this injustice is done, Bhaktin insists she will fight right up to the Viceroy. Perhaps some mothers have not done this when their children were jailed; let them do what they will, but she would have no choice in her action.

An encounter between two such contrasting contestants is difficult even to imagine.

I often consider that when the time comes for that call for which there is no opportunity to wash saris or pack luggage, no right for Bhaktin to tarry and no way for me to stop her, at the last moments of this eternal parting, what will this old villager do, and what will I do?

Bhaktin's story is still incomplete, but I would not like to complete it by losing her.

The Chinese Pedlar

It is difficult for me to discover distinct and memorable features which will distinguish one Chinese from another. Their identical flat faces seem to have been turned out of the same mould, and the pleat-like noses which break the monotony of their faces can hardly be differentiated. The neat outline of their slightly slanted, half-opened eyes, fringed with strange brown eyelashes, makes one wonder whether all these eyes have been cut out by a sharp-edged instrument according to the same fixed pattern. Their natural yellow complexion takes on the colour of dried red leaves lying covered with dust in the footsteps of the sun. Physiognomy, deportment and dress all combine to make these inhabitants of a distant land look like mechanically controlled puppets. That explains why, although I had seen a Chinese pedlar several times, it was difficult for me to distinguish him from others and remember him.

But today one Chinese with liquid blue eyes stands out in my memory from a maze of almost similar faces; his silent expression says to me, 'We are *not* carbon copies. I, too, have a life story and if your eyes are not ignorant of the alphabet of life, why don't you try to read it?'

It was many years ago. Alighting from a tonga I entered my yard and there saw a Chinese pedlar with a brown bundle of cloth hanging from his left shoulder. He was coming out of the gate, twirling a metal yardstick in his right hand. Perhaps, having found my house locked, he was going away.

'Will you buy something, Mem Sahib?' asked the unfortunate Chinese.

[25]

How could he know that this manner of address instantly arouses my ire. I have been called 'mother', 'elder sister', 'daughter', and so on, and I am familiar with all of these and like them. But this foreign mode of address makes me feel as if I have been shorn of my identity and as though my sari has been replaced by a dress. After having called me 'Mem Sahib' it would be positively difficult if not impossible for him not to go away disappointed. With contempt I replied, 'I don't buy foreign cloth.'

'Me a foreigner? But I come from China.' There was not only surprise but also pain in his voice at my slight. This time I paused, wanting to have a closer look at the man. Hiding his small feet in dirty white canvas shoes, wearing a lower garment which seemed a strange blend of trousers and pyjamas, and a jacket fashioned like a combination of coat and shirt, his hat half covering his forehead, with its frayed brim proclaiming its age, this thin, short-statured man without moustache or beard was the eternal Chinese. To see him as an individual entity – this was the problem that arose for me for the first time.

Thinking that my apathy had pained the foreigner, I tried to soften my negative answer by saying, 'I don't want anything, brother.' The pedlar turned out to be a strange person.

'You call me brother. Then you buy – you buy, yes!'

Finding myself out of the frying pan and into the fire, reluctantly I had to say, 'All right, show me what you have.'

Putting his bundle on the porch the pedlar said, 'Very fine silk I brought, sister. Chinese silk – crepe.'

It became necessary, after much interchange, for me to buy two table napkins. I thought it was good riddance, for with such a minimal sale it wouldn't be worth his while to come back again. But after a fortnight I once again found him seated on his cloth bundle on the porch, humming and tapping the yardstick on the floor. In order not to give him a chance to speak, I said in a peremptory tone, 'Now I absolutely will not buy anything, do you understand?'

Rising, taking something from his pocket and beaming with pleasure, the Chinese said, 'For sister I brought hankie – very best – all rest sold – hid in pocket.'

He held out a few handkerchiefs. Every corner crocheted with lilac thread, and every petal of the dainty flowers in the corners

embroidered with the same colour, expressed not only the nimble-
ness of Chinese women's fingers but also the pathetic story of life's
deprivations. Seeing my disinclination, blinking his blue, slit-like
eyes, he began repeating in one breath, 'For sister I brought – for
sister I brought.'

I thought to myself that I had acquired a peculiar brother. As a
child people had often teased me by calling me Chinese. Now I
wondered whether there had been some truth to their jibes. Otherwise how did it happen that this real Chinese had come to establish
brotherly relations with me, ignoring the rest of the population of
Allahabad? From that day on the Chinese pedlar acquired the
special right to visit my place from time to time.

Through the refined tastes of this pedlar, I began to realize that
even an average Chinese has a special affinity for art. Which colour
painting would look well on a blue wall, which designs of birds
would best decorate a green cushion, which flower patterns would
look well on a white curtain – in all these the Chinaman had the
same perceptiveness which can be found in any good artist. His
intimate familiarity with colour made me believe that even blind-
folded he would be able to identify a colour by mere touch.

Seeing the colourful cloth and paintings of China I began to
wonder whether every atom of Chinese earth was not soaked in
these variegated hues. Whenever I expressed the desire to see
China he would begin shouting, 'I go, too, sister,' and the azure of
his eyes would gleam with joy.

He was eager to tell me his life's story, but there was a consider-
able communication gap between the narrator and the listener. He
knew Burmese and Chinese only, of which I was ignorant despite
my learning. In the curious mixed language he used, of English
nouns without its verbs and verbs of Hindustani without its nouns,
the full pathos of the story could not be conveyed. But stories
which flow out of the heart, bursting its barriers in order to express
themselves, are invariably pathetic and the spirit of pathos
communicates itself despite inarticulateness. The Chinese pedlar's
story was no exception to this universal truth.

He was born after his parents had moved to Mandalay where they
had opened up a small tea shop. He had great reverence towards
the mother whom he had never seen; she had died giving birth to
him, leaving him in the care of his seven-year-old sister. Perhaps

a mother is the only being whom a person can remember as if there were nothing more to know, even if he has never actually seen her. This is but natural, for mother is the goddess who connects man with the world. By not acknowledging her it is possible to deny the world, but it is impossible to acknowledge the world and then to deny the mother.

After the father married another Burmese-Chinese woman and she began ruling the hearth, the tale of torture of the two motherless children began. Bad luck did not abate even with this, for the boy had hardly stepped into his fifth year when the father lost his life in an accident.

Like other innocent children, he had accepted the circumstances chance had brought him, but animosity between his sister and stepmother began to increase, due to the refusal of the sister to co-operate with a proposition put to her by the stepmother, and this poisoned his acceptance of his fate. In response to the adolescent girl's unco-operativeness, the stepmother not only took revenge on her but would also torture the brother. Many a time, putting his hands numbed with cold into the shivering fingers of his sister, hiding his tearful face in her filthy dress, he tried to forget his hunger by snuggling against her thin body. Often in the early dawn, while they stood shivering, with closed eyes, outside the locked door of the house, he leaned on the wall while trying to warm his frozen fingers in the sister's dew-drenched, dishevelled hair and he would ask his sister the way to go to their father. When in reply tear-drops rolled down the wan cheeks of his sister, frightened by the reaction, the boy quickly added that he did not want to ask the father for cocoa, he only wanted to see him.

Several times the sister fed the brother, obtaining cooked rice by washing dishes for the neighbours. The innocent boy could not know which particular pain was the last straw on the camel's back that broke the sister's resistance. One night, while lying in bed waiting for his sister, he half opened his eyes and saw his stepmother transforming his dirty and unkept sister as if she were a clever magician. On the sister's dry lips the stepmother's fat fingers were rapidly applying lipstick, on her wan cheeks she put pink rouge with her broad palm, the sister's coarse hair was braided by the rough hands and soon, pushing the girl outside, now dressed in bright-coloured clothes, the stepmother and sister disappeared into the darkness of the night.

The curiosity of the child changed into fear, and the fear into tears. At what point he fell asleep crying he does not remember. When he awoke at someone's touch, he saw his sister trying to control her sobs, kissing the forehead of her brother lying there curled up. That day he got a good meal, the next day he received some clothes and the third day some toys, but the chapped lips of the sister needed more lipstick each day and the waning cheeks needed more rouge.

He saw the wasting body and the increasing debility of his sister, but what he should do about it or to whom he should speak was beyond his comprehension. Repeatedly he would think to himself that if he could just find the address of his father everything would turn out all right. He did not remember what his mother looked like, but he did have a faint recollection of his father's appearance, and that memory convinced him the father had a loving nature. One day he resolved to himself that he would ask his father's whereabouts of every visitor who came to the old tea shop, and then one day he would quickly go to his father's place and bring him home. How frightened his stepmother would be, and how happy his sister!

Someone else was now the owner of the tea shop, but he was still sympathetic toward the son of the old proprietor, and so the child stood grovelling in a corner of the shop and in a stammering voice began asking each customer where to find his father. Some looked at him with surprise, some smiled at his question but one or two said something to the owner which made him grab the boy's hand and push him out, threatening to report him to his stepmother if he ever made the mistake of coming again. That is how the story of his search ended.

The metamorphosis of his sister each evening, her return after midnight dragging her leaden feet, his big-bodied stepmother jumping out of bed like a wild cat on soft paws, snatching the small purse from the limp hand of his sister, and the sister lying down, silently putting her lips to his forehead – the serial continued unabated.

But one day the sister just did not return. In the morning, seeing that the stepmother was somewhat anxiously searching for his sister, the child trembled with the apprehension of some unknown calamity. Sister – his only anchor – sister. He did not know the address of his father – now even his sister was lost. Leaving the house dressed as he was, he began distraughtly roaming the lanes in search of his sister. In the daytime it was difficult for him to recognize the metamorphosed sister of the night, so he ran from one side of the road to the other in order to be near any girl dressed in fine clothes. Sometimes he would collide with a person and somehow avoid falling, sometimes he was sworn at, and sometimes in compassion a passerby would ask how it happened that such a small child had gone mad.

Drifting like this, he fell in with a gang of pickpockets, where his education began. Just as people teach dogs to sit on their haunches, to stretch their necks and to salute by placing a paw near their snout, the pickpockets began coaching him in the art of crying, laughing and special gestures, meanwhile shutting him up in a room choked with smoke and stale air, littered with rags and broken utensils and packed with unwashed bodies.

Kneeling down like a pup he would practise different ways of laughing and crying. The source of his laughter had so much dried up that while trying to smile he would repeatedly make mistakes and get beaten. But his heart overflowed with so much sadness that even with a feeble attempt, two round tear-drops would roll from his eyes down both sides of his nose and, making parallel lines touching both corners of his mouth, would roll down below his chin. Taking this as an acquisition due to his superb teaching, the teacher, whose belly was black with a thick growth of hair, would reward him by jumping up and kicking him.

Reaching an age of greater understanding, he strenuously tried to locate his unfortunate sister but failed to find her. Lives of such women are not always safe; sometimes they are bought on payment and many times are simply kidnapped. Often, having lost all hope, they commit suicide, or sometimes drunkards in their intoxication will kill them. The initiator of the original mystery, the stepmother, had remarried and gone away to some far-off place to give happiness to her husband. Thus no way remained to continue the search.

In the meantime, the pedlar went to Rangoon on some business for his proprietor, then he lived for two years in Calcutta, and after that was ordered to come to this area with his other colleagues. He stayed at the house of a Chinese shoemaker and in the morning from eight to twelve and then again from two to six he wandered about hawking his cloth.

The Chinese pedlar had two ambitions – to be honest, which ambition was in his own hands, and secondly to find his sister, for which he daily prayed to Lord Buddha.

For months between his visits he would leave for other places, but on his return he would come to my house with some of his wares, saying, 'This for sister.' I had grown so much used to seeing him like this that when one day he began fumbling for words while saying, 'For sister,' not understanding his difficulty I began laughing. Gradually it transpired that a call had come and he would return home to China to fight. But where could he sell the cloth so quickly? By not selling and thereby causing loss to the proprietor he would be behaving dishonestly. If I could give him the required money and buy all his cloth, he could clear the account of his proprietor and would leave for his country immediately.

One day in the far past he had stood stammering as he asked the address of his father; today again he was stammering in diffidence. To gain time to think I said, 'No relation of yours is there. Then who called you?'

Filled with surprise, his eyes opened wide. 'When I say China not mine? When I say that sister?'

I felt ashamed of my own question. How could he be alone when the whole of great China was part of him?

It is difficult for me to keep money, and there was no possibility of my having a large amount immediately available. But I scrounged around for some cash, borrowed some from others, and thus made arrangements for the Chinese to go. He said his last farewell to me and as he briskly scurried away I shouted to him, 'Take your yardstick with you!'

Turning with a smile he could only say, 'For sister – '; the rest of his words were lost in stammering.

Today many years have passed and there is no possibility of my seeing the Chinese again. I have never been introduced to his sister and yet both the brother and sister refuse to fade from my memory.

From the bundle of the Chinese I have utilized many bolts of cloth to have kurtas made for the village children, but there are still three bolts in my wardrobe, and the yardstick rests in a corner. Once, seeing these bolts, a lady friend of mine who was fond of wearing handloomed cloth reproached me by saying, 'There are those who outwardly say we should support our village handloom industry and yet secretly buy bolts of foreign silk. That is why our country is not progressing.' I could restrain my laughter only with great difficulty.

There is no proof that the orphaned Chinese brother, unhappy from birth, separated from his sister, had the satisfaction of reaching the only foundation of his life, China – but my heart hopes he did.

A Pilgrimage to the Himalayas

(THE HILL BOYS)

As I turned away from the labour contractor, he was compelled to
stop bragging about himself and end his long drawn out recital of
the characteristics of the men who worked under his thumb. Still
clutching in my hand the receipt he had given me scribbled on faded
manila paper, I turned to look at the evening sky which now glowed
like the final bright burst of a flickering oil lamp. When, despite a
bout of loud coughing, the old man failed to pierce my apathy, he
placed his pen, whose nib was clogged with dried ink, behind his
slightly protruding right ear and, holding the lidless ink-pot filled
with watery ink in his gnarled fingers, he slowly descended the
steps. As he turned away, coolies began congregating in front of my
room.

These coolies, who belong to the tribe of Dotiyals, are a strange
lot. Coming from Nepal and Bhutan, their personal merits are
judged solely on their load-bearing capacities. Even the scrawniest
among them is able to lift a load of from one hundred to one
hundred and fifty pounds, and with it on his back climb the miles-
long ascent of the towering mountains. In appearance they somewhat
resemble those who were in Lord Shiva's marriage procession,
though Shiva's processionists were ugly in aspect but not humble
in deportment, whereas the Dotiyals have boundless humility and
are less repulsive to the eye.

Some seem like ambling bears dressed in weird trousers of jute
cloth and shirts resembling woollen pillowcases made from torn
black blankets of rough weave. Some, hiding their private parts

[33]

with scraps of cloth and string and wrapping their torsos in thread-bare cotton jackets with thick load-bearing ropes tied around their waists, look like porcupines as they scratch their unkempt, stiff, dry hair. The calloused heels of some, with their flattened and twisted toes, rival the hardness of an anvil, while the feet of others seem like claws clamped in shreds of handwoven coarse grass mats.

Basking their naked bodies in the sun and picking lice from their tattered apparel, they remind one of monkeys; and after having groomed their bodies with oil they shine like amphibians emerging from water. We acknowledge them as human beings perhaps by sheer habit and not because we identify them with recognizable humanity. Seeing this crowd of remarkably strange faces, my aunt withdrew into our room, and Bhaktin stood on the doorstep, surprised at this picture of poverty and peculiarity far beyond anything seen in the villages of the plains. Seeming somewhat despondent, she looked at them and began sizing them up. I said, 'All of you go away. My coolie will be Jang Bahadur. Send him to me.'

Hearing my words they looked at one another, and a bolder one among them said, 'Ma'am! *He* is Jangia.' I did not immediately realize that Jangia was identical with Jang Bahadur and once again said, 'Call Jang Bahadur.'

Surprised by my response, they began elbowing each other. Then a man pushed another in front of him and said, 'This one calls himself Jangia.'

Seeing a man devoid of the attributes of the much praised coolie of the contractor, I suspiciously queried, 'What is your name?'

He shot back the answer, 'Jang Bahadur Singh.'

On hearing the name it became necessary for me to look carefully at the man. Incessant tramping on the meandering rocky footpaths of the high Himalayan mountains had left its mark on him in the form of broken toe nails and injured toes splayed apart by sandals made of coarse wild grass. His condition seemed to mock the God who, having made a human being into a pack animal, had neglected to bestow cloven hoofs on him. Jangia's trousers, made of several cotton and woollen pieces stitched carefully together, hung to his knees as if jeering at man's quest for modesty. His jacket, given to him once upon a time by an unknown person, had become thread-bare, exposing a filthy lining. It made the person wearing it seem more animal than human. His unkempt hair, popping out of the holes of a cotton cap of unidentifiable form and colour, reminded one of seaweed peeping out here and there in muddy water.

Beneath thick eyebrows his nose was slightly rounded, and below it the face was somewhat broad. His inveterately grinning lips almost touched his ears, shortening the distance between them. His sparse black moustache, like fine black threads creeping down below his lips, seemed to be trying to disclaim his baby-sized teeth. Watery little eyes gave his broad face, hemmed in by a narrow forehead and stunted round chin, the liquidity of a pond in a desert. His brown complexion, having been exposed to inter-mittent sun, had groves of freckles and patches of rusty copper hue. One end of the knotted rope used for tying luggage circum-navigated his neck and was clinging to his shoulder like a garland; the other end was wrapped around like a waistband and played hide and seek with the spots on his tattered jacket. That is what Jang Bahadur Singh, alias Jangia, was like. He, along with his cousin Dhan Singh, were to carry my luggage to Badrinath Temple via Kedarnath, and then back to Srinagar. One rupee a day was to be paid to each of them, out of which one tenth was to go to the contractor,

'Where's your cousin?'

As I asked, a chorus of voices began reverberating, 'Dhania! Dhania!' but even when pushed forward by the others, he stood recalcitrantly behind his cousin. Without anyone telling me, I realized this must be Dhan Singh. His deportment reflected extreme reverence toward his elder cousin. The appearance of the rounded, somewhat muscular Dhania was also in tune with his deportment, for the fine lines of his brown eyebrows and his rather pointed short nose expressed his simplicity as well as his sharpness. The right edge of his lips was slanted a bit upward, creating a frozen laughing expression on his face.

His clear complexion and smoothness of skin indicated that he had not yet undergone the full hardships of the life of a coolie. His old jute trousers and jacket of torn denim gave him the air of a defeated soldier, in contrast to his cheerful facial expression.

The thought struck me that on the meandering footpaths of the mountains the lives of myself and my fellow travellers would be in the hands of these guides, and that they would be under my

protection for their meals and daily necessities. This unexpectedly
roused my motherly feelings towards them. I said, 'You take a
look at the luggage, and if you think it is too heavy, I will hire one
more person.'

Jang Bahadur, followed by Dhan Singh, stepped into the room
and began assessing the bundles, easily lifting them one after the
other. Bhaktin and my aunt were amazed at the ease with which
they hefted the bundles.

I have walked long distances on the mountains, and the key to
success in these wanderings is to carry minimal luggage, so I had
not made the mistake of having huge quantities of baggage. I also
do not see any sense in carrying cans of butter and cartons of
biscuits when it is possible to get food on the way. The wish to
eat canned butter and dry biscuits under the shadow of beautiful
snowy peaks is beyond me. I have particularly enjoyed baking
potatoes and chappatis by scavenging dried cow-dung cakes and
twigs for fuel, and lighting it in the shadow of the peaks. My aunt
was, of course, eager to carry more articles but, agreeing to even
my small whims as was her wont, she also had brought only light
luggage. Since her sons were not able to take her on such a pilgrimage and I was the one escorting her, in her eyes I had become
equivalent to her eldest son and she therefore had full faith in
my wisdom.

Accordingly, I had only a few clothes for all of us, some bedding,
a medicine kit, soap and a few other necessities. Jang Bahadur
agreed to take them without additional help and the next morning
our pilgrimage began.

On such pilgrimages, the passing view one gets of others reveals
far more of their true nature than one is normally able to uncover.
Inside his own home a person can hide his true self in his dealings
with his family and servants, and can more readily dissimulate. But
it is not so simple on these arduous pilgrimages. Innate selfishness,
boorishness, cruelty and apathy are quickly revealed in a person's
manner of paying his coolies and deciding about their meals and
rest breaks. When fellow travellers need comfort and help, the
occasion will invariably give us a glimpse of the inner self, making
it possible to divine true character.

While tramping, one sees, clearly visible, snow-clad mountain
ranges appearing like rows of half-opened, white lotus buds and

slowly melting away from view in the mist and cloud; sometimes there are vast stretches of green valleys and flowing streams of molten silver water – these awaken more sadness in me than happiness.

Sitting on a dandi carried by two coolies on their shoulders, some pot-bellied man exhorts the panting coolies to walk faster. On another dandi, a lady from a prosperous family, beautifully attired, ignores the beauty of the mountains and prefers to doze. An old woman with head shaved and body like dried wood jogging along on the coolies' shoulders looks only at the road with an annoyed expression, wondering when the journey will end. Sometimes one sees a man seated in a wicker carrier strapped to the shoulders of a coolie, dangling his feet while his eyes turn upwards in prayer. A bit ahead is a brave man straddling a pony, reminding the animal's keeper not to pull its tail since it makes the beast panicky. Sometimes a monk seated in a dandi appears as greatly pleased as if he had already arrived in heaven, when he looks back at the streams of his followers behind him carrying conch shells and monastery flags.

Besides those travelling in dandis, wicker carriers and on ponies, there is another group – the poor people. Lacking money, some of them become expert at riding trains without paying the fare. Hiding a minute amount of money on their persons and carrying cheap snacks of jaggery, fried gram and flour, they join the pilgrimage. Knowing that they probably lack sufficient means to survive on the high mountains, they begin their journey only after taking leave of everyone. If they fall sick on the way, their companions will leave them to their fate and move on, for if all stay for a few days their meagre supply of food and money will be exhausted and none of them will reach their goal. They decide among themselves before leaving that if one of them is not able to reach the temple, it will be because of his sins. But if others are also prevented from attaining this goal due to one man's sickness, then the onus of the first man's sin will also be suffered by them.

At each resting place, one or two among them are bound to fall sick, and sometimes they die. The last ceremonies for the dead are performed after begging money for the rites from other pilgrims. If this is not possible, the corpse is simply thrown into one of the deep, ever-present ravines.

Among the pedestrians, one occasionally also sees tourists. But they are fully equipped with the necessary travel paraphernalia and they walk only for pleasure. Most of them hire ponies who are ordered to trot sometimes ahead of them and sometimes behind. No one speaks to the poor pilgrims – neither the people who ride in dandis nor these fashionable tourists.

Death visits the caravans of dandis also, but it is confined to the coolies only. If a coolie catches cholera or fever or gets severely injured, he is left behind to meet his fate. Another coolie is engaged to replace him and the pilgrimage goes on. If the sick coolie survives he goes back to the starting point and searches for another pilgrim. If he dies, there is no dearth of ravines in which to discard his corpse. Luggage-carrying coolies of the pilgrims in dandis have to run beside their customers, and this really exhausts them.

The pilgrims who ride ponies drive them as relentlessly as the proverbial two-wheeled coach-owner of the plains, who buys a pony for twelve rupees and then makes it run day and night so that he can collect triple his purchase price as quickly as possible; when the exhausted and broken pony dies, the owner still shows a profit even after purchasing a new animal.

The pilgrim who walks also hires a coolie for a rupee a day and is therefore eager to cover three days' journey in one, so that he is not the financial loser.

A pilgrim who just sits in his dandi and yawns has a stock of dried fruit and snacks, so there is no possibility of his getting particularly tired or hungry, but he keeps on reducing the rest and meal breaks of the coolies. In the morning the coolie is ordered to cover twenty miles by evening and he must cover this distance otherwise his wages will be reduced. So these helpless people gasp for breath at the high altitude, foam oozing from their mouths, and keep running.

It is ironic that at such heights it is really the coolies who are all-powerful, and if one of them would scowl, look at the pilgrim and then glance downward to a point hundreds of feet below in a deep ravine, the dandi rider would surely faint. But how can they risk showing annoyance?

We, too, wandered in the midst of these heavenly ranges, having to ignore the death and sickness hidden in the purified air of the Himalayas. I will not ride on a dandi, and the others also walked with me.

Nothing is more contagious than human emotions, and Jangia and Dhania became our compassionate guides. Today I cherish their memory as the gift of my pilgrimage.

They had two pieces of jute cloth for bedding and a torn black blanket which was so short and narrow that if it covered their legs their torsos were bare, and if their heads were covered their feet would naturally pop out. Even though dressed in filthy clothing, their sense of religious purity had not deserted them. Far away from the village at the place where we would rest at night, they would discard their clothes and with a piece of cloth covering their private parts would, like holy men, solicitously watch their rice cooking. Despite my best arguments, I failed to persuade them that in the absence of a second set of clean clothes which would meet religious standards, their alternative of cooking naked was a sure invitation to pneumonia.

They each had a steel pan: in one they would cook lentils and in the other rice. Sometimes, to economize on lentils, they would collect some wild green edible grass which grew near streams and, boiling it, would eat it with their thick and half-cooked chappatis. Except for potatoes, no vegetable is available in the mountains but, feeling that this wild grass was fit only for wild people, no one else would eat it. Once, on their insistence, I ate the greens, and after that it formed an important item of our menu.

Walking behind them on the road, we could see only their legs, their bodies being hidden beneath the loads strapped to their backs. Dhan Singh's legs would rigidly follow in the footsteps of his cousin, though he was so shy that he dared not look straight towards us. On steep ascents, whenever the weight of the load would begin shifting from their toes to their heels, and their feet would slip back, I would realize without looking at their faces that they were tired. But when I asked, 'Are you tired, Jang Bahadur?', the familiar answer would reach me in local dialect, 'I'm OK, Mother,* No trouble.' This manner of address did not amuse me because of the serious tone in which it was spoken.

---

*The word 'Mother' is used by the hill boys as a respectful and affectionate form of address which really has no modern English equivalent.

I have been called 'mother' from a very young age and have received affection accordingly, but the gentleness and the easy acceptance of motherly affection which was apparent in the speech of these hill boys is difficult to find anywhere else.

Dhania, due to shyness, would not raise his head. But Jangia would often turn around on the way and inquire about our needs and physical condition. Then one day, as if asking for an invaluable thing, he spoke with utter humility, 'Mother, if you walk ahead of us it would be better. Turning my head to look at you hurts because of the load. If you walk ahead, I will just raise my head and see you walking, and then my steps will also become brisker.'

After that we began walking in front of them.

Arriving at Adi-Badri, Dhan Singh lay down in the corner of the room where we had paused for the night, and high fever gripped him. I gave him some homeopathic medicine from my kit, and after giving him a cup of specially brewed tea Bhaktin began feeling herself to be an expert nurse. Seeing Jang Bahadur crouching humbly, I told him to massage the feet of Dhan Singh in order to assuage his pain. He replied with his usual diffidence, 'I am older, Mother! He is shy – I couldn't do that, it's not right!'

Hearing these words about decorous behaviour, I was naturally taken aback. An old mother of a respectable family once told me that now and then her son raises his hand against her, and on being reminded that she gave birth to him the brat replies, 'The days are gone when you got your feet worshipped. You bore me for your own pleasure – so why should I spend my life worshipping you for that?' When people have become so callous towards their own mothers, talk of proper behaviour toward a cousin seems futile.

But Jang Bahadur's younger cousin was old-fashioned and therefore to have his feet massaged by an elder seemed to him against etiquette – it need not surprise us.

When a coolie falls sick, the pilgrims won't tarry on his behalf; engaging another coolie from the nearest village, they move on. The prevalence of this behaviour provided an occasion to know the extent of my bearers' pure, lasting affection which might have been difficult to ascertain otherwise.

Jang Bahadur knew that in place of his cousin another coolie would be engaged, but he also knew that if he left Dhania behind and went ahead, he would not be able to face Dhan Singh's mother.

Being sick, Dhania could neither return home nor recover lying there alone in the room. If they stayed on for a few days, all the money they had would be gone and the prospects for another load were uncertain. Under the circumstances, the elder man could not leave his younger cousin without deviating from his duty. He therefore decided to call two new coolies in the morning and stay on to look after Dhania.

Dhan Singh, even without hearing the decision from the lips of his brother, had intuitively grasped his decision. He had realized that his cousin would not be able to leave him and also that he would lose his wages. Whatever little money they had would be used up in buying medicines, and after that it would be difficult to wait for another load or even to return home. He resolved to get up in the morning and somehow carry the load.

In the morning when I returned after washing my face in the stream, I saw Jang Bahadur waiting for me at the lower end of the village with two new coolies; near the room Dhan Singh, tying a band of cloth on his head, was adjusting his load.

When I asked, 'Are you well?', wiping away his perspiration he replied only, 'I will go.'

This glimpse of affection between the two cousins left me tongue-tied for a few seconds. On hearing from me that I would stay on for two or three days and then travel with them, their faces glowed with surprise. Somehow, I felt sad and repentant. Man's misbehaviour toward other human beings is now so common that its absence is surprising. Dhan Singh recovered on the third day, and the following day we resumed our journey.

Their behaviour toward one another and their mutual empathy could not but arouse my respectful affection for them, which only increased as we travelled further. Some of my books, the medicine kit, pots and a few other articles were heavy and each would try to take them in his own load to lighten the burden of the other. In the morning each one would try to get up earlier so that he could take the opportunity to tie all the heavier articles in his load. Even if I gave a single piece of candy to one, he would run to share it with the other. One would call to the other if he saw a vista or an object worth noticing. They were like two children whom some fairy had instantly raised to manhood by her magic wand.

They were also sympathetic and kind to the other coolies walking on the road. Once a cow skidded while coming down the road and her hoof hit the leg of a coolie and it started bleeding. Entrusting his load to Dhan Singh, Jang Bahadur carried the injured coolie on his back up to the stream and, after I had dressed his wound, he again carried him piggyback to the next village. Then he had to return and carry his own and the injured coolie's load also to the village. By that time it had grown dark and he had to wash the blood stains from his tattered clothes while shivering in the cold. But the questioner would get the same answer from his lips, 'No trouble, Mother! I'm OK.'

Dhan Singh was shy and did not talk much, but Jang Bahadur would occasionally sit and narrate sad and sometimes happy incidents about the village, his home and his parents.

He was the youngest son of a couple living in a sparsely populated village of Nepal, and as there was no other means of livelihood, from childhood on he had been coming here with other coolies. They came at the beginning of summer and went back as autumn descended. Some of them would be hired to carry luggage to Lake Kailash, deep in Tibet, some to Pindari Glacier, and some to the holy temples of Badrinath and Kedarnath. A contractor had the name and number of each coolie and if someone did not return and there was no information about him, he was assumed to have died. Similarly, if he did not return to the village nor send any information through others, the members of his family assumed that he had departed from this world and by observing proper ceremonies would at least try to make his path to heaven smoother.

Jang Bahadur had been in trouble many times, because in order to earn more he not only undertook to carry luggage to distant places, but also made several trips in the summer. Due to his precarious life, parents of marriageable young girls had not considered him fit to marry their daughters, but two years back he had escaped from the curse of remaining unmarried. The parents of the bride were already dead and her relatives decided that whether the boy died in the snows or returned home very rich, in either case his family would have to be responsible for the girl and keep her with them, and so they married her off, absolving themselves of their sacred duties.

Last year Jang Bahadur had not come here to work, but this

year the fields had not yielded much and his wife had borne him a son, so it was necessary to earn something.

When he left his home his son was two months old, but he was so emaciated and tiny that the father dared not take him in his arms. Now he was hoarding the wages left after meeting his meal expenses to take home, and if he managed to get some tips his ambition was to get a cap and kurta sewn for his son. His young wife had repeatedly implored him, while humbly holding out the folds of her sari in front of her, tears flowing from her eyes, to go only with a respectable person and not to climb more than once with a load. His father, placing hands behind his back and looking toward the sky with brimming eyes, had invoked the mercy of God on his son. The mother had followed him to the edge of the village, crying and beating her head. Despite his assurance to her, she would not go home, and stood beside a decrepit old tree gazing at his diminishing silhouette, as if trying to retrieve him with a rope of her tears.

The parting was almost an annual ritual, but this year a distraught wife and silent son were also there to share the grief. Considering Jang Bahadur very reliable, his widowed aunt had made her son accompany him. That was why he now always searched for a pilgrim who would engage both of them.

This was my second trip to Badrinath, and I had decided not to go to Kedarnath for I wanted to arrive in as short a time as possible at the heavenly city ensconced on the banks of the roaring Alaknanda river. But when I returned to Rudra Prayag and, standing on the banks of the Alaknanda, saw Kedar mountain like a flower caught aloft for a few moments in the sweeping winds of a storm, I regretted my decision. Only those who have seen Kedar mountain standing as if in deep meditation, its foundation hidden in multi-hued flowers, surrounded by the waters of five streams, its peak pointing into the blue void, canopied by white snow, can realize its attraction. From miles away its white peak is clearly visible and silently beckons you. As you approach, it looms ever larger, its silver-white shimmering silhouette becoming more pronounced. On the trip home, when it disappears from sight, a strange feeling of loneliness overwhelms you.

After reaching Rudra Prayag, some of my friends were so tired that they could not undertake another stiff climb. Badrinath peak is only five miles away from Kedarnath as the crow flies, but it takes nine days to cover the distance by road. Perhaps the Hindi saying, 'To cover five miles in nine days', has arisen on this road.

When I resolved to go there, some of my companions agreed to wait for me at Rudra Prayag and also to take rest there, thus killing two birds with one stone. One coolie was adequate to handle the baggage of those who were going to Kedarnath. The question then arose as to what to do with the other coolie. My own predilection was for the other coolie also to take rest along with the others, and on our return to Rudra Prayag after eighteen days, all of us could go down together.

But how could Jang Bahadur accept eighteen rupees without working for the money? Very shyly, as if asking for a boon, he told me that he now knew Mother and could entrust Dhan Singh to her. Therefore he would go down to Srinagar, look for a new pilgrim, and wait there for Dhan Singh. When all had returned, he would travel again with Dhania.

One may not compose a poem about Jang Bahadur's self-sacrifice but its memory does evoke a poetic feeling in me. When I ordered Jang Bahadur to accompany me and Dhan Singh to take rest at Rudra Prayag, he chuckled with delight and his eyes became wet with tears. Taking courage in both hands he had proposed his return to Srinagar, but really it was difficult for him to bear the thought of separation. Much later he said in his simple way, 'I didn't cry in front of you because I was shy and I respected you. But I went a little apart and wept loudly. When I thought about how Mother was going away, my insides were all shaky.'

This pilgrimage also one day came to an end, and, putting us on the bus, the cousins stood there looking lost. Trying to hold back the tears Jang Bahadur said, 'Mother, live long and come again. Send a letter in Jangia's name.' Dhania was as usual looking shyly toward the ground, bidding farewell with great tears rolling down from his eyes.

Where the two hill boys are today I do not know. But the feeling I got by being their 'mother' is difficult to communicate.

Munnu's Mother

While walking through the village of Arail for the first time, I saw a ruined building made of bricks, in strange contrast to the mud huts which usually abound in villages. Out of curiosity, I asked a woman who was sticking cow-dung cakes on an unplastered wall near the door to dry them for fuel, 'Could you please tell me who lives in this house?'

The one to whom this query was addressed, making her rasping voice still more astringent, almost barked, 'What is that to you? Do city women have nothing better to do than loaf around?'

Dubri's wife is a shrew and has a reputation for her lashing tongue. One or two dirt-embedded wisps of her very unkempt hair brushed her scaly lips. Her dark body, entombed in layers of dirt, had become so filthy that it was impossible to distinguish it from the muddy sari she wore. Every finger of the hands which were daily smeared with cow-dung told a tale of quarrels. She believes in gaining friendship through quarrelling, since if she is not defeated in a battle of wits, she feels it below her dignity to even talk to a person. And anyone declining her challenge is straightaway dubbed as unworthy of her friendship.

I was not then familiar with this aspect of her temperament. Besides, I am really not surprised by such curt responses, for due to poverty and a myriad of unsatisfied wants, peevish characters abound in the villages. And furthermore, Arail is known to nourish habitual criminals, so few people go there expecting pristine kindness. I knew that an equally harsh reply would evoke the response

[45]

of a steel arrow striking against a rock. Therefore it took me a few minutes to think of a negotiatory reply.

But for Bhaktin not to reply to such provocation would be as contemptible as running from the battle field, and she retaliated immediately, 'There is an uproar in the city; people are saying that the queen of this village is collecting cow-dung and patting it into cakes. We have come running to have an audience with her. Is it clear to you now why we are here?'

As if to prevent a flare-up at this curt response, a medium-statured, thin woman emerged from the door of a mud hut near a small temple on the next hillock. She was wearing a cotton sari whose faded red colour now rivalled the hue of ancient clay tiles that have absorbed layers of dust. Drawing the sari's edge up to her eyebrows as befitted a shy young woman, solicitously and softly she inquired, 'What is your question, ma'am? Have you come from the city to see Arail village?'

Between these contrasting responses, you can image my predicament; and just as a pendulum pulled to one side swings back to the opposite end, the reaction of Dubri's wife quickly drew my feet to the cow-dung plastered mud platform which stood in front of the hut of Munnu's mother.

It would be incorrect to dub Munnu's mother ugly, but on the other hand, to proclaim her beautiful would be at variance with truth. She is not beautiful to look at, but her heart and her mind are beautiful, and one intuitively feels this. Because of a dark complexion and wan cheeks, her plain face looks rather elongated. Except for its aquiline hook, her stunted nose would have led one to think of her as stupid. Her eyes are neither large nor small, but are lit with a strange luminosity. Thin lips, when they reveal the small white teeth, somehow express happiness, but when they are closed they convey an indefinable sadness. Her legs and hands are coarse in comparison with her facial expression. Her elastic body stands erect like an arrow except for a slight bend of her head.

Nickel bangles, flattened and worn down, obviously fitted on her when she was still a child and not taken off since, tightly girdle the ankles of her short legs; her feet are replete with sores. Chipped and dirt-encrusted glass bangles worn around the flat wrists of her stiff-fingered hands seem as if they were on the wrists of the wearer when she came into the world.

Like all the brides of the respectable families of the village, Munnu's mother is soft-spoken, shy and devoted to her duties, but in this wilderness she is like a wild flower blooming amidst disdain and anonymity.

By assiduously plastering the open courtyard of the house I use in Arail with cow-dung, Munnu's mother has made it so attractive that this doorless habitat is now more valuable to me than a fine house. Even now, she shuffles restlessly as if reflecting the unspoken yearnings of the ruins.

Looking at the child Munnu, I felt as if his mother had somehow salvaged a segment of her dissolving life dream and hidden it beneath her blouse. Chubby round face, almost globular eyes and an arched nose make him attractive. His precocity and sharpness belie his five years and it makes me sad that in the future his only scope will be in the world of crime.

They were so poor that even the acquisition of clothing had become a luxury. Sometimes Munnu's mother would sew a long, oddly cut kurta out of old clothes, or out of some new piece of rough cheap cloth, and would then lecture the child so much on the need for keeping it clean that he now believes his kurta to be more valuable than his own naked body. It may be raining, storms may be thundering or hot winds blowing – he will take off his kurta and, tucking it in a safe place, venture to play with his friends. And when after playing he returns home naked with the kurta tucked under his armpit, he looks like a mannikin made of the black soil of the River Yamuna, able to breath due to the power of a magic incantation.

Besides them, Munnu's father and his old grandfather were the other two inmates of the household.

Munnu's father is slim, of medium height, and has a wheat-coloured complexion. The short hair on his head is always standing upright and is obviously ungroomable. There are dark patches under his eyes and freckles on his cheeks, and magnifying their ugliness are the pimples which adorn his face.

Everything about his face gives the impression of being out of tune, but what is specifically so is difficult to pinpoint. It simply hasn't the gentleness of pleasant thoughts.

Leaving his bed in the morning he walks over to the other side of the hillock and, squatting beneath the peepal tree, whiles away the time by smoking and feeding his pet partridges. Then at ten he picks up the leather flask of mustard oil from its spider-web-covered niche in his unventilated dark room, and vigorously applies oil to his body. Then his bath in the river Yamuna is also a long-drawn-out affair. Returning, he will eat fried gram or whatever is available, but only after rebuking his wife in exchange for the meal. Thereafter, if he succeeds in wheedling some money from his wife or begging some from his old father, he hides it in the folds of his loin cloth or, failing that, leaves without money and goes out in search of gambling friends.

His return late at night heralds the fact that he has made gains in his profession and so he does not care about meals. But if he comes back by early evening, obviously he has suffered a loss; then, adopting a posture as if he were obliging the others, he eats his sparse meal and immediately falls into a deep slumber, lying on the bare broken cot, to rise only in the morning. This is how he whiles away his time every day.

His mother died when he was still a child and his father reared him up in his arms with great love, hence his name Hathai, the hand-reared one. If the father's love, besides raising him, also strengthened his evil mind, well, one can only suppose it was a quirk of fate. In the end, thinking that to suffer alone the rigours of his evil fate was an act of cowardice, he brought home a simple, hard-working orphan girl as his bride.

The old father, a peer among high-caste Brahmins, castigates as modern heretics those who do not believe in the dictum that begging is the rightful profession of Brahmins in the current evil era. From early morning on, he sits on the bank of the Yamuna river facing the holy confluence. Spreading a dirty, torn towel in front of him and placing by its side a broken tumbler, he narrates his sad story to the passing pilgrims in bits and pieces – a portion in his wobbly voice, some of it through trembling hand gestures, and some through the expressions on his wrinkled face.

His audience, all of whom are engrossed in their own sad plight, hardly have a moment to listen to another's story. They try instead briefly to grasp its import and, just as during festivals when the religious discourse and stories are over devotees throw rice, coins and flowers with hands clasped before them, so now the pilgrims take a handful of the cheap rice, gram or barley brought with them and throw it on the towel spread in front of the old Brahmin, hoping thus to attain religious distinction. Some reckless ones, dropping a small coin or two by mistake in their hurry, just walk briskly away. Seeing them rushing along one cannot but think that, despite having taken several dips at the exact confluence of the two holy rivers, they really have no faith that thereby their sins will be washed away. They intuitively know that their sins, having stepped aside while they were bathing, are coming running right behind them and the moment they tarry the sins will climb back on their shoulders. In the meantime, the doing of charitable works is meant to divert the attention of their immortal and perpetual shadows. These diversionary efforts, however, are also hit or miss affairs. To avoid raising the questions of why, what and to whom they should give, they concentrate on training their eyes not to really see what they are looking at. Fingers entangled in a string of clattering holy beads, lips and tongue muttering incantations which they do not understand also fulfil the same purpose.

The old man, the despised but main witness to this great dissimulation, ties together his collections at about one in the afternoon and returns to his hole-like home. The daughter-in-law either simply boils the mixed grains collected from begging, or separates them and cooks their rare meal of rice and lentil curry.

Not infrequently the grains thus obtained are insufficient, and Munnu's mother goes out to work in someone else's field, barn or house. In the evening, collecting the grain paid to her in lieu of wages, she trudges toward home with heavy footsteps and aching hands, and reaching there she begins to undertake the chores of a housewife also.

Taking an old earthen pot and a remnant of some happier days, a copper vessel, she goes to the river Yamuna to bring water. Returning, she picks up the earthen lamp from the niche on the wall above the mud oven and, blowing off the ash from the half-burned wick made of an old piece of cloth, she soaks it in oil begged from someone and lights the lamp. Then she begins igniting the fuel in the oven. By picking up cow-dung from footpaths and fields and patting it into cakes, and collecting dry twigs from trees, she continues to solve the problem of fuel supply.

If she is given millet or maize, she first puts a pot with water on the stove to boil the lentils, and then, by rotating the bamboo handle of the worn-out stone grinding-pan, set in a dark corner of the house, begins grinding the seeds. In between she has to get up to re-kindle the smoking fire, to light the hubble-bubble of her father-in-law, and to give fried gram to Munnu to assuage his gnawing hunger until the milled flour is made into chappatis. In her situation she has to live from hand to mouth, and her household resembles that of a wandering gypsy. But she skilfully does not allow the indeterminate livelihood to become really painful.

Sometimes, having collected everything together, she will find that there is no salt in the house, so depositing Munnu on the door-step she runs to the village shopkeeper. When the smoke from the burning cow-dung cakes begins to choke her unbearably, propping the half-baked chappati alongside the mud oven away from the fire so it does not burn, she will run out and bring in dried reeds or castor-oil plants to feed the fire. Sometimes, while eating, her father-in-law will ask for chillies and she will reach for the row of broken pots kept in a corner. She never worries as to how and from where the next meal will be coming, as by now she has acquired the knack of meeting unexpected demands.

Owing to her hard work, none goes to bed hungry; off and on they are even served special meals. By churning the buttermilk of some neighbour she will earn a tumblerful, and grinding gram and peas with it she will cook karhi. Sometimes after working in a sugarcane field she will coax some juice from the owner, or even the dirty froth of the boiling juice, and this mixed with cheap boiled rice will make dessert for the family. Helping the vegetable seller carry her load to the market, she may get a few pieces of vegetable as a reward, and cooking them will render the ubiquitous lentil curry more palatable. Running her household requires the adroit-ness of a chess player; making one mistake could cause the whole arrangement to break down.

The father-in-law is often down with a cough, and then old age itself is also a disease. For ten to twelve days in a month he is prevented from begging. On the remaining days also, he sometimes indulges in activities which others might consider useless but which are rather significant from his point of view. When some coughing and spitting old crony of his appears for a bout of smoking, his getting up without consuming not only his own stock of tobacco but also that borrowed from others would be the height of bad manners according to him. Sometimes the memory of an old co-worker makes him so restless that, donning his torn, padded jacket kept carefully on the cot and hiding his tobacco and snuff pouches in the folds of his loincloth, he will begin walking to his friend's village with bamboo stick in hand. Finding a co-operative listener from a nearby village, it would be a betrayal of his wisdom acquired through age not to narrate the story of his better days. Duties like these are numerous and, according to him, must be performed.

And now, since the daughter-in-law has begun sharing the chores of earning a livelihood, freed from anxiety and lying leisurely on the broken cot, he will expound on the virtues of rendering service to others in a harangue directed to Munnu's mother. Firmly believing that one reaps what one sows, he directs no wise words to his son, but exhorts his daughter-in-law to earn queenship in heaven by being a virtuous and devoted wife.

According to the old man, life here is too short but not so the life after death; by suffering in this short life, living in a hole-like mud hut, she could earn the queenship of heaven. By feeding her father-in-law and his good-for-nothing son with chappatis browned in the smoke of dried castor-oil plants and by grinding gram and barley in the worn-out stone grinding-pan she is obviously the eternal beneficiary. Travail of a few days here in exchange for a pleasurable abode in heaven for eternity – where is the clod who would not agree to this bargain? Millions of people in this world are able clearly to perceive with their sharp eyes the fine advantage concealed in this future barter, so obviously there are very few fools in this world.

The old man is not less proud of his own intellect. By marrying off his good-for-nothing son to a useful bride, he demonstrated that he was a manipulator of the calibre of the ancient God and not even a whit less in intellect, otherwise the playful God would surely have made him renounce the world and become a holy man, there being no one to look after him in his old age and therefore no other alternative. Now, thanks to his brains, by becoming the grandpa of Munnu he has escaped from this trap and eats meals not only cooked by his daughter-in-law but also earned by the sweat of her brow, so that he can proudly sit smoking on the rough cot with its three and a half legs.

It would also be a grave injustice to dub the son as a good-for-nothing when his manliness has procured such a hard-working and well-behaved wife. Acquiring a wife and begetting children are the pinnacles of a man's ability. So why should he who has reached these goals try to carry the load of additional abilities? Therefore, from pure pragmatism also, the idle life of Hathai is not useless. His father has succeeded in cleverly providing for his own and his son's livelihood, thus erasing the fate lines ordained by the creator. If God does not aim his death shaft at him and spares his life a little longer, he could also make provision for his grandson, and only after partaking of the meals cooked by his grandson's wife will he proudly leave for his heavenly abode.

The life story of his daughter-in-law is similarly unusual. Her father was a penniless minstrel of holy fables and a dispenser of religious discourses in a village near Rewa. Her mother had died when she was still a small child and the father brought her up. Tucking in one armpit his holy books wrapped in red cloth, and in the other the child dressed in a bib, he would go even to far-off villages to give religious discourses and narrate holy stories for the benefit of the credulous people.

Seating his daughter in a corner, he would try to demonstrate his learning by reading aloud correct and incorrect Sanskrit words, but from time to time he would not forget to glance at the offerings of coins placed near the idols of the zodiac and at the yawning girl seated statue-like there. Tying the dry sweetened flour offering in a torn dirty sheet and holding the panchamrit in an earthen cup, sometimes he would not return home until late in the night.

If the offering was adequate, they would both partake of it there and then, and thus be done with their meal. Otherwise, on reaching home the child swallowed the sweet flour with panchamrit and went to sleep, and the father would lie down on an empty stomach.

Poor and motherless girls somehow grow up fast. Necessity and inborn womanly instincts conjointly spanning the years give them understanding far beyond their physical ages. Butia had been doing small chores since the age of six, but when she stepped into her seventh year she began looking after the household completely.

With repeated trips she would replenish the big water pot by filling a small tumbler; outside, she would scavenge for dried twigs and cow-dung for fuel; kneading the wheat flour loosely, she would somehow bake burned chappatis.

It would be wrong to say that she did not suffer while doing these chores, but the happiness of helping her father outweighed these travails. Sometimes her knees would get bruised while she tried to pluck twigs from tall shrubs; while carrying water she would stumble and hurt her toes and sometimes her fingers would get burned while baking chappatis. Somehow bottling up her welling desire to cry, she would apply mustard oil to the bruises and soothe the burned fingers by bandaging them with dough.

Her father was now very proud of his daughter. His Butia was able to manage the household – what more could he wish for. Whenever he went out to narrate his holy stories, Butia, in order not to lag behind, would follow in her father's striding steps, trudging on her short legs. Reaching the place where the listeners were, she would arrange before her father the holy artifacts that were required for the religious discourse and would remain awake, seated in the corner like a statue until the discourse was finished. She did not yawn any more, and would listen intently, pleasantly surprised at the vast learning of her father, her hair standing on end as she brooded over the characters in the holy stories, thinking about which one she would like to be.

Walking back home, the father would carry the holy books and the pot of panchamrit, and the daughter the load of coconut, betelnut and sweetened flour tied in a sheet. At this time she would ask so many questions concerning the characters in the narratives that her father would be pleasantly surprised at his daughter's precocity. But in this process he would sometimes grow sad. If his Butia had been a boy, he would have made him the best narrator of religious tales in the world, but a daughter was like money in trust – she had to go to someone else's household, and the best he could hope for was her marriage into a prosperous family. Even for this he would only have his lucky stars to thank.

But before he could return the trust, the summons arrived which no one has the power to refuse. When he lay dying from fever, an old fellow student providentially arrived who had renounced the world after the demise of his wife and, shaving off his hair, had become a holy man. In the absence of any relatives, the father entrusted the care of his daughter to the wandering man and promptly died, to recite his life story in another world.

Nine year old Butia, despite her precocity, did not know much about life and death. As there was no one else in the house to shed tears over her father's death, she could easily be persuaded that her father was only sleeping and she willingly went away to a neighbour's house to play. Returning and seeing the empty house, she began crying and then even the reassuring voice of her new uncle could not restrain her. She did not fully believe the explanation trotted out to her that her father had gone to see a doctor. Several villages beyond, a doctor friend of her father used to live; therefore the story did not appear impossible, but her father had never before gone anywhere leaving her behind, and this made her doubt what she had been told.

Later she came to know everything but, crying bitterly over the loss of her father, the sole companion of her lonely life, she began zealously serving her new 'uncle'. Harsh by temperament, his behaviour was devoid of any empathy and could not fill the void left by her father's death, but wise Butia concealed this from her new protector.

Fond of wandering about, he proposed to sell the family mud house so that they could go away to some far-off place. Restraining her tears with difficulty, she nodded agreement. In the mud house, filled with memories of her father, she had not felt lonely. Every day she would bathe his idol of Lord Shaligram and then return it to its usual place. Wiping the holy book with the edge of her sari and tying it in the well-known red cloth, she would hang it from a peg. Plastering with cow-dung the corner where her father used to sit and worship the idol of Lord Shaligram, and spreading the mat of wild reeds, she would imagine her father seated there.

But how could she insult the trust of her late father by going against the wishes of the uncle to whose care he had entrusted her at the time of his death? One day, therefore, tying in an old sheet her father's holy books, her childhood toys and one or two cooking pots, she left her familiar village, trailing in the footsteps of her new uncle.

Her house was bought by some merchant, but for how much and what happened to the amount received, only her uncle knew.

It may be possible to inquire what she did not encounter in the course of her gypsy-like life. To ascertain what she did see is futile, because obviously she saw and suffered much.

In the course of these wanderings, at the time of the Magh fair, when people congregate for a ritual dip at the confluence of the holy Yamuna and Ganges rivers, her guardian stumbled into Prayag and, boarding a boat, alighted on the banks of Arail. People say that he had come to the fair with the idea of selling the girl, but how far this is true or merely imagined is difficult to ascertain. At the time of the fair, a pilgrim landing on the bank has to pay two paise as toll tax. The uncle did not have the money and he started prevaricating. Probably seeing his discomfiture and the frightened looks of the young girl who had been brought against her wishes, the toll collector abruptly asked, 'Where have you kidnapped this girl from?' Now, due either to a guilty conscience or some other reason, when he left Butia there, supposedly in search of a shopkeeper to change his note, he just disappeared and has not returned even to this day.

The unfortunate girl, getting tired of waiting, put her head on the bundle of her meagre possessions and began wailing. Then people on the bank took notice of her. Arguing intermittently about laws and police regulations, they discovered a Brahmin family who were willing to take the girl, and thus absolving themselves of their duties, they did not consider it necessary thereafter to find out what had happened to the girl.

In the new house, putting her father's holy books in a nook and placing the idol of Lord Shaligram in the row of deities adorning the family temple, she again began her career of service.

The daughters of the old Brahmin were already married, and his son and daughter-in-law were aspiring to the status of respectable old people. The orphan girl became their unpaid serf. Impartially she began undertaking all the chores of the household. She had not only to wash the holy utensils and scarf of the old Brahmin, she even acquired the duty of massaging his wife's back and tightening up the strings of her bed. She used to pick lice from the hair of the daughter-in-law and also sew for her.

It was her duty to light the hubble-bubble of the son and to polish his leathery shoes with mustard oil. She had a sterling character and, like gold, the heat of sorrow made it shine even more and did not turn it into dross.

In the meantime, Hathai's father saw this hardworking well-behaved and soft-spoken girl and, despite not knowing her parentage, proposed marriage with his son.

There was nothing else at her father-in-law's place except these two mannikins of bone and flesh, and she had to content herself with the gift of a scarf and some glass bangles; the old cotton skirt of her dead mother-in-law was the other addition to her wardrobe. Dressed in this old and new apparel, with glass bangles around her wrists, a thick line of vermilion colouring the centre parting of her tightly drawn-back hair to show her married state, and a narrow crown of green paper and tin foil adorning her head, she reached the doorstep of the dark mud house of her father-in-law. In the house, equipped with broken earthen pots and peopled by spiders, rats and lizards, she found no one to welcome her.

The ladies of the neighbourhood greeted her and, having her sit on a torn mat, explained to her the duties of a bride and then departed for their castles.

The old Brahmin lady had sent a basket of fried wheatcakes and sweets along with Butia. She was not hungry and did not eat anything, so her father-in-law and husband had a hearty marriage meal.

Tired Hathai, lying in the corner dimly lit by the flickering earthen lamp, was soon snoring. Butia, too, crouching near his feet, slept through the night.

Rising in the morning, Hathai went away in search of his friends, and the father-in-law, before starting for the banks of the Yamuna, coughed loudly and said, 'Daughter-in-law! Take care of your house. I am going!'

The daughter-in-law had a close look at the house and taking a broom swept away the spiders, crickets and other prowlers; by the time the old man could return with some rice and lentils, she, having already polished the house with cow dung, had returned home from bathing in the Yamuna.

Putting rice and lentils in a lidless cooking pot and covering it with a broken tin plate, she began cooking kichri while the father-in-law, seated on the doorstep, narrated the story of his better days. By then, whistling and holding a leaf cup of cheap sweet noodles in his hand, Hathai had also arrived. Excavating some powdered tamarind from a broken earthen pot, and grinding it with salt and chillies, she produced a sauce. Spreading the tattered mat on the floor for the father-in-law to sit on and putting beside it the dented tumbler with Yamuna water, she jingled the iron door chain, inviting the smoking in-law to have his meal. In a leaf cup she served them left-over wheatcakes and the sweet noodles brought by Hathai, and gave them kichri on the broken tin plates. When she sat down to watch them eating her heart was suddenly suffused with unexpected mother-ly feelings: that house with the two male inmates was a vivid illus-tration of the Hindi proverb, 'Ghosts move into the house which has no mistress.'

In the same mud hut, worrying and fussing over the two peculiar creatures, she had grown from a thirteen-year-old girl into a woman of twenty-three, from newly-wed bride into a mother. Her worries had now reached the breaking point, but no one had the time to spend a moment thinking about what would happen to her.

In the ruins we stumbled on to one another, and with the passage of time our acquaintance blossomed into a lasting relationship. When I summoned Munnu and his mother to the city for the first time to see an exhibition being presented, she showed up dressed in an old sari washed with saltpetre, holding Munnu's hand whose nakedness was wrapped in the torn, discarded cotton towel of his grandfather. Entering the living room they thought it was the exhibition and began bowing to the statues kept in the room. In the evening, when they were actually escorted to the exhibition by Bhaktin, they were literally overwhelmed by its dazzling beauty.

Since then, on occasion Munnu's mother will announce that she intends going to her mother's place, and comes to the city. My house is the only place she can call her own, and this thought makes me sad.

With the shortage of grain in the market, prices went up and the question of earning a livelihood became even more acute. Some-how persuading Hathai, I sent him to a nearby fort to do some work, but he did not stay on. The fact is, he hasn't the desire to work, and when he does earn some money he gambles it away.

So it happened that one day Munnu's mother hesitatingly asked me for some job in the school and, despite my repeatedly telling her that I would be happy to maintain them throughout their lives, she would not agree to come to the city without having some job to do. Finding no way out, I arranged a less arduous job for her. But taking it easy was not her style. Every day she would go out with the bullock cart and calling the girl students from their houses would return with them in her cart. The rest of the time she would either be stitching a padded jacket for some bullock cart driver or a mattress for some maid, and if there was nothing else to do she would sweep and clean every nook and corner of the house. Munnu, after eating, would put on his new kurta and trousers and either write the Hindi alphabet on a slate or play with the cat and dog. Sometimes he would just sit on the doorstep of my office.

In the night, both mother and son would spread a drugget near my bed and go to sleep. She was not willing to change her habit of sleeping on the floor.

I had thought her days of drudgery were finished, but this did not turn out to be so. One day, drawing the edge of her sari shyly up to her eyebrows, she told me that she wanted to go back to Arail. She reported that the old man was not getting his meals for days on end because Munnu's father would disappear periodically, and her visit to Arail every ten days was not enough, since without her the household could not be managed. I realized the truth in her words, and arranged for her return.

This time I was not able to visit Arail for a long time, and when I did get there I found that arrangements for the annual festival of bathing in the river were in full swing. Not seeing Munnu's mother in her hut, I enquired as to her whereabouts. I was told that she now went across the river each day to work. There ground was being levelled for the fair, and many men had been employed in this labour. She, too, was engaged in transporting earth in a wicker basket on her head. During the day she got an hour's break, but how could she return home? The boatman charged two paise for each crossing and, as it was, four paise were being spent daily so that she could cross morning and evening. Going home during the break would double that expense. So she carried earth on her head the whole day in the sun on an empty stomach, and in the evening, after buying flour and lentils out of the wages she earned, she returned home when the village was already lit with earthen lamps. Since she was a Brahmin, she could not carry cooked food to work and, besides, it would be difficult not to get her meal contaminated by the touch of low-caste co-workers.

That she, being a Brahmin, should carry earth on her head was neither palatable to others of her own caste nor to her family. But she would not listen to any arguments against it. The question of her hunger affected only her, and that is why she did not insist on carrying meals with her nor incurring the expense of coming home during the break; but the lives of many people depended on her wages and she could not agree to let someone else make the decision about this. Having grown up with hard work, she accepted the alternative of carrying earth as being better than survival by begging – this was her helplessness. But if the society which revels in following the beaten tracks of custom were to allow such a display to grow unchecked, not one acceptable social norm would remain. That is why a Brahmin woman working was like poison to the society of beggars and egocentric Brahmins.

In the evening, covered from head to toe with dust, Munnu's mother returned and, lighting the earthen lamp, went to bring water from the river. Coming back, she set the pot on the mud oven to boil water for lentils and then came to greet me.

Due to her work arrangement, Munnu was in great difficulty, since in order to protect him from the dust and give him a chance to eat she would leave him at home. She would either bake chappatis the previous night or at five in the morning, and leave them for Munnu. After eating with his grandfather or father, the problem of what he should do for the whole day was hard to solve. Sometimes he would go with his grandfather to the bank of the Yamuna, or play with vagabond boys. At other times, sitting under the peepal tree, squinting his eyes he would try identify his mother in the crowd across the river. He would become utterly despondent, wondering what could be happening to his short, thin mother, when even very tall and muscular men seemed to shrink to the size of crawling insects when they crossed the river. Fortunately, on reaching his side of the river she would again become the same smiling mother. He had questioned the tallest man, Thakur Dada, and also the shortest boy, Nanhku, about why people became so tiny when they got across the river, but no one understood the significance of his curiosity.

Whenever I arrived at Arail, the boy would be with me constantly, and the attributes of his temperament became known to me.

The boy is clever. His way of looking at many things and giving opinions about them is different from that of other boys. One day, observing the train running on the bridge over the river Yamuna, he exclaimed, 'Look! See the row of lights rushing away!' On persistent questioning, nodding his head like a wise person, he would agree, 'That was a train with lamps lit, going away!' In the night, the silhouette of the train traversing the bridge does melt away in darkness and it looks like only a row of lights rushing away. This is true, but who will not be surprised at hearing the poetic description from the lips of Munnu. He is fond of music, also. He not only remembers hymns heard here and there, but also tries to sing them with the same pitch and melody. Being shy, he is not able to demonstrate his full learning to me. Beginning and stopping several times in a recitation, when he finally accepts defeat and exclaims, 'Do you know why I forget everything in front of you?', it is hard to keep from laughing.

Watching children loafing about in the sun and women quarrelling without any reason, the idea came to me to open a school in which women during their leisure hours could learn weaving and spinning, children reading and writing, and old people could listen to the newspapers being read. There may be a difference of opinion in Arail as to the need for opening such a school, but if an idea strikes me, I have to execute it.

In a few days I succeeded in collecting the spinning wheels, looms, books, and other necessary articles. A full-time resident teacher was required as I could only come to Arail one or two days in a week. This problem was also solved.

Due to old age Bhaktin was becoming feeble, and I had engaged Anurup as her assistant. Observing his knowledge of the alphabet and desire for learning, it seemed right to educate this cowherd boy, Anurup. When he succeeded in getting a diploma, it seemed appropriate to entrust to him work of more responsibility than that of a mere assistant to Bhaktin. Giving him crash training in the science of teaching, I made arrangements for him to stay at Arail. An old lady who knew knitting and weaving was also willing to live and work there.

But spinning wheels, looms and other articles could not be kept in my doorless room, and all the houses in the village seemed hardly large enough for the needs of their inhabitants. To buy new land and a house was beyond my means.

Then I remembered the vacant brick house whose rear mud portion used to collapse during the rainy season with monotonous regularity. I was informed that the owners had not lived in the village for twenty-two years. In winter, during the annual festival of bathing in the river, some of them would come to the village for a few days and then the smoke of burning cow-dung coming out of the cob-web-covered chinks looked like the sighs of the ruins. The rest of the time the house just stood there motionless, seeming haunted. The caretaker liked the proposal and the future students, who currently had no other recreation than playing in the mud, embraced the corroded walls of the house and began calling it their school. And when the caretaker informed me that the house belonged to the poet Thakur Gopal Sharan Singh of Nai Garhi, I hired some men to clean it up and wrote to the owner about my venture.

I had no doubt that he would agree to my request, but when his reply came dubbing my utilitarianism as futile activity, I was more depressed than surprised.

Now I have more experience of the ways of the world. What can one say to famous artists, even those who can rhyme a few lines or imagine a small incident, who don't concern themselves with utilitarian social activities? If all artists were to waste their time trying to improve the living conditions of the disinherited poor people, when would they get leisure to write immortal epics?

I sent the spinning wheel to another village, gave the books to another person, got the old lady employed somewhere else, and fulfilled my promise to Anurup by getting him a job in the Education-expansion Department of the school system.

Even now I still return to Arail and, sitting in my room, listen to the songs of Munnu and the life story of his mother. The brick house standing there proclaims the hollowness of authority, and the ruins of its mud portion disinterestedly listen.

Some child emerging from around a corner suddenly says, 'You have been away a long time, ma'am,' and someone else enquires, 'When will our school open?' In reply, I feel like screaming, 'You are unfortunate children. Your village is a criminal one. Your progenitors and their ancestors have acquired this reputation and have ruined their lives. Now you also gamble and learn thieving. But no one should try to interfere in the rights of people to do what they want.' But the surprised, frightened gaze of the liquid eyes beneath dirty eyelids and muddy eyelashes makes me sad and tearful, and without looking at anyone I step forward toward my boat.

Grandpa Thakuri

Bhaktin would not believe me when I told her of my resolve to observe religious anchorage during the coming Kumbh fair and that I planned to live in a specially constructed hut on the opposite bank of the river Ganges. In one breath she shot out many questions, attempting to awaken me to my lack of foresight; how could I teach and then return each day to the hut, what fares would the tonga driver and boatman demand, and many other such puzzles.

She is fully aware that once I have made up my mind it is futile to argue with me since this only steels my determination further to go ahead with my plans, but she is helpless to control her tongue. When, despite her torrent of questions, I held back any reply, she poutingly spoke up: 'What's your hurry? Have you taken some kind of oath to fulfil all your religious obligations right now? There will be time enough to observe anchorage when you grow old!'

My plans had not been made for the sake of observing rituals, but it was difficult to make Bhaktin understand this. Therefore, in order to avoid the labour of futile explanations, I confirmed her fears of my folly by keeping quiet. She knows that my uncommunicativeness is a sure sign of my firm resolve to do what I want to do. She is thus far more apprehensive of my silence than of my arguments, for while we are arguing there is some chance of a change of view, but no hope at all when I lapse into silence.

So in the end, despite the advice and views of a counsellor like Bhaktin, bundles of reeds, bamboo and other materials began to appear on the steps of the ancient Samudra Kup temple and labourers began to construct my hut. In the centre, a neat ten by ten foot room was built, and surrounding it was an eight foot wide verandah. The north end was designated my study and the south end a kitchen for Bhaktin. In the south end she hung sacks of sattu and jaggery from the ceiling and improvised a strong rope hanger to keep her saris and mattresses on. The door of the centre room opened toward the east, therefore the eastern verandah became the living room in which I met visitors. When everything was ready, Bhaktin's coarse drugget and my finely woven mattress, her dim smoky kerosene lamp and my flickering light in the bronze lamp stand, her battered buckets and my copper water pots gleaming flame-like, her earthen pots filled with basics like turmeric, spices, flour and lentil, and my Sanskrit books filled with spiritual knowledge – somehow all these made my hut look lived in.

That is how Bhaktin's and my anchorage began. Around us there were also other huts, but they were so tiny that one could barely turn around in them.

Some time in the past these anchoritic congregations must have been significant social events and one can imagine this by observing even the present ceremonies. Perhaps they were an important means and occasion to create meetings between people living in different parts of this sub-continent, for the formation of individual friendships, the exchange of views, and as a cultural matrix. The mighty rivers of India have been life-sustaining, and it is no wonder that these meetings were formed on their banks. Today we have forgotten the original whys and hows, and observance of petrified rituals has become our religion.

I like to participate occasionally in such living because the amount of insight I gain about life there would be difficult to gain in so short a time otherwise, and then, too, perennial curiosity about life has become part of my nature.

When, during the rainy season, mango stones which have been discarded after their juice has been licked away begin sprouting, I care for them more lovingly than any professional gardener would do. When a bird nests in some corner of my house I am her most careful watchman. Many such birds and wild plants survive and grow because of my compulsive love for life and strange fascination with the vigour of the life-force. A cactus whose milk causes blindness even at a touch grows lustily, raising its proud head by the side of a carefully nurtured mango plant. Wild shrubs, whose thorns once having pricked you are imbedded forever, grow proudly alongside pearl-like cobs of corn covered with silk skeins.

Many a time, unable to resist the pain in the steady small eyes, I have had to pick up and bring home whimpering stray pups found shivering on the streets in the bitter cold. The gasping of a fish in the net just pulled out of the water, the fluttering wings of birds crammed in the narrow cages of the bird seller, and the pathetic howling of panting dogs locked inside the iron-grilled cage of the dog catcher – all of these have frequently inspired me to undertake strange activities.

If such an odd duck were not beholden to human life, it would be a matter for surprise; if her thirst for knowledge regarding happiness and pain, life and death goes beyond normal limits, this seems easily understandable.

But unfortunately Bhaktin has to do all the unusual chores resulting from my natural inclinations. After sweeping twigs and droppings fallen from the bird's nest perched high on the trellis near the roof, purifying herself she will stand facing the sun and give an offering of water – at that moment the pup will make the courtyard dirty. Washing the ground and again bathing, she will proceed to offer water to the idol of Lord Shiva and will then hear me asking her to give some jaggery and sattu to the beggar waiting on the doorstep. Performing this duty also, she will sit on her haunches. Closing her nostrils with her right hand she begins mouthing holy incantations until I shout for her to come out and accompany me on a visit to a sick friend. But even living under these disorganized conditions, she does not complain. Sometimes, indeed, pursing her lips and feigning seriousness she exclaims, 'Why is there no exam measuring my job skill? If there were, I would also earn a diploma in my old age. Isn't that so?'

Despite not having a diploma, Bhaktin knows the importance of her duties. That is why even when she is only slightly ill she wails anxiously, 'When I die, what will happen to her? Who will cook for her and see that she eats? What will become of her zoo?' Her stepping down from worry about dying to worry about the care of my menagerie makes me smile.

Because of her deep faith in religion, anchorage is very significant in her eyes, but she knows that my habit of collecting all kinds

of odd family members will give her no respite and that there will
be no opportunity for her to break out of the bonds of worldly
illusions. To me, village fairs and anchorage are equally good
schools of learning but I somehow study only to strengthen the
bonds of earthly attachment and not for the purpose of
detachment.

The evening before Sankranti, the main day for bathing in the
river, as I began reading Patanjali's *Yoga Shastra*, strands of
clouds began coalescing, as if woven through with the flashes of
lightning. Bhaktin had just lighted the oven when a bevy of village
pilgrims invaded the kitchen. Because she is so obedient to my
wishes, she becomes a tough opponent for the rest of the world, and
there was no way she could excuse this sudden invasion.

Flashing out like a storm from her kitchen corner, she exhibited
her skill in throwing arrows of choicest vocabulary which she
reserved for such occasions until I had to get up myself to see what
was happening.

Emerging, I saw a crowd of children, grown men and women, led
by an old man. How this disorganized group of visitors had gate-
crashed on to my verandah loaded with their large and small
bundles, pots, hubble-bubbles, mats, baskets, buckets and ropes,
was not at all clear to me.

On seeing me, Bhaktin's countenance, livid with rage, began
instead to show signs of guilt and her thundering voice receded
into a whimper; probably the visitors immediately understood
that I was the sole owner of this reed shanty.

Taking a few steps toward me, the old leader spoke in a serene
and affectionate voice. 'My queen daughter, will you not allow us
poor pilgrims to stay here? We have walked a long way. This
world is transitory – everyone leaves when morning comes – isn't
that so? The monk of Samudra Kup asked us to stay there, but I
would have a long climb each day down to the river, and would
have to climb the hill again to sleep – too much for an old man like
me. And there is not even a place to sit on the sand, it is so crowded.
It's getting dark – where can I go? What am I to do?'

The old man's voice and his intimate way of speaking somehow
irresistibly attracted me. Ignoring the language of refusal written
plainly in Bhaktin's eyes, I replied, 'You may stay here, grandpa.
This room is big enough for me. If necessary Bhaktin can cook

outside. The verandah is quite large and all of you can live there. Of course this world is transitory!'

I went into the room carrying my mat and books and, lighting the lamp, started reading. The visitors arranged their bedding.

Bhaktin quarrels with others for the sake of maintaining my comfort, but once she realizes that the person's activities will not inconvenience me, her truculency melts away. The crowd might have disturbed my peace – this possibility had hardened her attitude. But when this fear disappeared she was as soft as usual. She began rearranging the oven of bricks and stones in a corner beneath a sack of sattu hanging from the ceiling, thus releasing space for the invaders.

That night I did not see my uninvited visitors. The next day was a holiday and, while I am not modern enough to forgo bathing at the confluence of the holy rivers, neither am I so old-fashioned that I feel it necessary to earn religious distinction by bathing at the appointed time, pushed about by the surging crowd. So in the early morning before the sun had even risen, waking Bhaktin, I walked toward the Ganges as she lay rippling beneath a thick layer of mist.

When I returned, the golden rays from the east were criss-crossing the thick fog, and it seemed as if someone had sewn perforated lace of golden threads on the white sheet of water.

My spacious, peaceful cottage located to the right of the steps to Samudra Kup was today unrecognizable. The chaotic world located within it gave the impression of the normally peace-filled heart of a great yogi in which a waft of uncontrolled passions had entered with one negligent and unregulated breath. Coming closer to the hut I took a careful look at these peace disturbers.

The old man, with the ostentation befitting his status as leader, had occupied my study-verandah. A torn drugget of unrecognizable colour, with a woollen shawl wrapped around it, was placed there. By its side, lest it feel lonely, a bundle tied with a torn and dirty piece of cloth was also very much there. The hubble-bubble made of black coconut with its red mud fuel container was leaning against the bamboo pillar. A black cotton tobacco pouch with edges laced in red strips of cloth was hanging from the reed wall. On the string stretched from the pillar to the wall a loin-cloth and cotton-padded black jacket were hanging as if proclaiming the glory of the owner.

The big bamboo stick was so shiny from having been annointed daily with oil that even its knots appeared smooth. Just on the outer edge of the verandah his wooden sandals with thick cotton straps showed that the owner had made a compromise between the unacceptability of leather shoes and the hardness of village wooden sandals.

I almost believed that the old grandpa had spread his belongings about so ostentatiously in order to overshadow the exhibition of my books. He had perhaps gone in search of a twig of the neem tree with which to brush his teeth, and like a spy I assessed the sources of his strength now on display to the world.

In the other wing of the verandah the crowd was rather strange. One blind man was seated as if in a trance. The pockmarks on his face gave a clue as to how he must have lost his eyesight. The tense, protruding neck veins on an otherwise emaciated dark body indicated that he worked out his anger against his blindness through his neck. While the reed walls were being erected, one edge of the supporting bamboo pillar had somehow been left sticking out like a peg, and now a fiddle and a pair of small cymbals hung from it. He also had a sheet, a jute mattress and a very much dented water pot with its sharp edges curved inward from much rubbing and cleaning. Beyond the jute curtain of that verandah an elderly man was seated on the sand in lotus fashion and had opened a coloured box made of reeds. The dab of sandalwood paste on his forehead proclaimed that he was a Brahmin. The reed box seemed to be the prison in which either Lord Shaligram or Lord Shiva were kept, and probably he was removing the stone used to grind sandalwood and the half-ground piece of sandalwood from on top of the idol in order to ease the pressure on the god. A book of prayers to Lord Hanuman was placed on top of a bundle of holy books which rested on a length of cotton cloth emblazoned with the name of Lord Ram; obviously the god's divinity had to struggle daily with the demonic power of ghosts.

Two adolescent boys shivering in a black blanket perforated with countless holes were trying to mitigate the pain of the cold sand beneath them by precariously sitting on one edge of the jute curtain. One of them was gazing hypnotically at the sack of sattu and jaggery hanging from the ceiling, and the other looked at the Brahmin's activities with surprise and seemed to be trying to understand their meaning.

A middle-aged man was sitting in the sun with a tattered old sheet covering his emaciated body, but his jutting angular shoulders and dry hands with their swollen veins were readily visible. His mud-spattered feet covered with sores seemed sturdier than the rest of his skeleton. Like a scribbling child, fate had written so much in the language of wrinkles on his forehead that it was now difficult to decipher.

The financial condition of the women folk seemed equally lean. Two old women with prayer beads in their hands were seated on the cold floor, leaning on a huge bundle. One of them was yawning. She had tubular bangles tightly girdling her ankles and flat silver bangles around her wrists, demonstrating her persisting love for ornamentation despite a shaven head. The other appeared more conscious of the world around her. She had a black thread around her neck with two pendants of the seeds of the rosary tree, perhaps worn in the ornament-wearing tradition of women. In the facial expression of one there was pathetic sadness, her dim eyes covered with film and her nose bending toward her chin. The other women, ears peeping outside her sari, lips opening and closing, small black eyes revolving, the round nostrils of her stunted nose dilating, seemed to be trying to identify and feel the beauty, essence and smell around her. Nearby, a large pumpkin with a sickle propped against it showed the love for food which these two ascetic women had, and the smoothness of the black earthen pot of ghee which hung in a sack from the ceiling was in clear contrast to their outward roughness.

I could not see the face of the elderly woman dressed in a well-worn sari with patches of white lace. Having untied the rope from the bucket used to draw water from the well, she was in a corner trying to stretch it into a clothes line. The woman standing nearby with a load of old torn clothes, waiting to spread the rags on the rope, somehow especially attracted my attention. Not only the muddy sari with red border whose edge she had pulled over her head and down to her nose, but also the red glass bangles around her wrists, the somewhat loose and thin ankle bracelets and the rings on her toes denoted her married status. The unsymmetrical broadness of the face which showed beneath her veil had such a gentle expression that though one's eyes could not call her beautiful, neither could the heart decry her as ugly.

By her side were two dark adolescent girls occupied in rummaging through the contents of a big reed box. Like an alphabet of poverty were the tangled dirty plaits of hair hanging down by their round faces. On the other side, on a piece of torn drugget, a dark girl dressed only in a tight ragged shirt was sleeping. Her frequent shivering indicated the fierce struggle going on between the cold and her desire to sleep. Another boy sitting with his back resting against the bamboo pillar rubbed his eyes and seemed about to cry. In the absence of a shirt, his torso was wrapped in a threadbare old scarf. His eyes lingered on the earthen pot hanging from the ceiling and on the bundle on the floor and he finally burst out crying. Obviously the pangs of hunger were now gnawing more than the cold outside. In the eastern corner, on a pad woven of rice stalks, the drawn-up knees of the sleeping figure covered by a muddy sheet showed that he had passed the cold night shivering.

One dark-limbed woman was digging a hole in the sand as an improvised oven. The small nose-ring on her long face with protruding attenuated bones was trembling and would sometimes touch her lips or upper cheeks. The black cotton lace on her long red skirt had frayed off in some places. The weakness of her anaemic body, clearly visible through the old yellow hood, was belied by the swiftness of the hands digging a hole for the oven.

Putting two fingers to her lips, Bhaktin murmured in surprise, 'Oh God! The whole fair has come to our place. Now who would want to leave this zoo and go and see the rest of the fair?'

Eyeing Bhaktin wrathfully, I was thinking up an excuse to begin talking with my visitors, but I was a little startled by the easy approach of one of the veiled women: 'I touch your feet, elder sister. We've given you a lot of trouble.' What reply could I give in response to such an address? Even my urban suavity could not think up one, and trying to follow the tenets of good manners I merely said, 'No trouble – on the contrary, you are inconvenienced because of lack of space.'

Then I went to tidy up my room and Bhaktin, after preparing cheap rice, lentils and sweets of jaggery sprinkled with black sesame seeds, went out to observe the ritual of giving a food offering. Returning, she cooked our meal, a mixture of boiled rice and lentils.

I like to tease Bhaktin when I am eating, since at no other time will she try to flatter me; on the contrary, on other occasions she is always ready to browbeat me.

Sweets of sesame stewed in jaggery being very sweet, I do not care for them. That is why Bhaktin instead serves me sweets of crushed sesame mixed with a small quantity of white sugar. This time, Bhaktin had given away all these sweets to beggars and Brahmins, and nothing was left for me. Sensing this shortage, with a serious visage I said, 'Bring some sweets for me!'

But before I could enjoy watching the discomfiture of Bhaktin, yesterday's familiar voice broke in, 'Queen daughter, can I come in?' I do not observe untouchability, and Bhaktin was safe within her thick coal circle, so hearing, 'Come this way, grandpa,' the old man presented himself with two leaf cups in his hands. The crown of his head was smooth and shiny due to baldness, but a few lingering strands of white hair still clung to the back of his head as if, afraid of the hard lines of fate on his forehead, they had run away to the rear to hide. In his small eyes there was a strange reflection of mixed sadness, thoughtfulness and affection. Elongated wrinkles running from both sides of his nose were lost in the maze of his beard. The sentimentality of his lips was overshadowed by the thin line of moustache, and his unusually broad face was made to look normally proportioned by his beard. In his thick beard, a few black hairs amidst long white strands looked as if in a mesh of silver filaments some black threads had got entangled here and there. Owing to his general alertness, one's attention was not drawn to the weakness in his physique; similarly, one did not notice his height, as he stooped a little while walking. With shoeless feet and loin-cloth hanging to his knees, he was like any other old villager.

The grandpa had brought for me some sesame sweets, ghee, a whole pickled mango and yoghurt. Despite my repeatedly telling him that I don't like to eat ghee and for health reasons do not eat chillies or pickles, disregarding my protestations he put ghee on my food and the pickled mango on the side of the plate. Propping the leaf cup of yoghurt on the edge of the plate, solicitously he cajoled, 'Taste a little daughter! Do educated people live on such meagre fare?'

From that day on my specific acquaintance with the visitors began, which soon turned into affection born out of our living together so closely.

Every day, at nine in the morning, I had to cross the Ganges and then go to the university in a two-wheeled horse carriage. Not liking to travel alone, I compelled Bhaktin to accompany me on these journeys. By the time I was free to return, Bhaktin, like the mythical sage Narad, would already have listened to the life story of the coach driver and pronounced judgement on his mistakes, or, talking with acquaintances, would have solved the problems of the world.

Because of the rush in the morning, no proper arrangements could be made for meals, and naturally it took some time after returning to prepare a snack. I do not know how and when my country visitors sensed this predicament, but daily, as I stepped into my hut, several new items of food would invariably be offered to me. Each person would save something for me and keep it safe in the hanging sack. I would be offered corn porridge topped with thick milk in a big metal cup; on a small metal plate I would receive sattu, jaggery or pua, and in a multicoloured reed basket some fried grains or baked sweet potato. And despite my protestations that if I ate all that food my health would be ruined, they would insist on my eating.

'Sister, won't you just taste it?'; 'You just touch it with your hands, queen daughter, and my heart will be satisfied'; 'Elder sister, put a bit in your mouth, then all this labour will not be wasted.' Hearing such pleas it became difficult to decide which one to turn down. Reluctantly, I had to eat everything from fried gram and jaggery to pua made of corn and other village preparations, despite my differing urban tastes.

Thereafter, they would troop down to the bank of the river for the ritual evening bathing and offer lighted earthen oil-lamps to the river. And, like an eager and curious observer, I would follow them.

Anchorites eat only once a day and, despite the cold of December and January, will not make a bonfire for warmth. These rules were framed partly due to the cost of fuel, partly because of the shortage of grains and partly in response to the tradition of penance.

But in winter I enjoy sitting near a huge bonfire and watching it. For me there was no shortage of dried cow-dung cakes and wood, so I would light a big bonfire in front of my cottage and, sitting on a stool brought by my visitors along with their household articles, I would enjoy the warmth. Their children, who were free from the rigorous rules of anchorage, and Bhaktin, who is more preoccupied with this earth than the world beyond, would sit near the fire and warm their hands and feet. The true followers of the rules would maintain a minimal distance between themselves and the fire so that the accountant in heaven, Lord Chitra Gupta, who records the sins and pious deeds of individuals, could be deceived into believing that they were really observing the ordained rules.

In the evening they would have varied activities. One would sing a hymn and another narrate a mythological story. Sometimes new interpretations would be offered of a popular saying or comments made on current problems. These villagers had equal command over the mystic utterances of the poet saint, Kabir, and practical tips on how to buy a bullock; their company was never dull or useless. Due to this constant exposure, I gradually became familiar with their life stories.

Old Grandpa Thakuri belonged to the caste of bards and was therefore a born poet. Since I am also a poetess, both of us could be said to belong to the same caste. In modern times, with the break-up of the feudal system, a lot of change has come about in the duties and utility of these professional poets. Now hardly anyone is aware of their existence, nor do they understand the worth of their professional expertise as poets. The inherited professional skill is utilized now only for their individual pleasure.

Sensing the trend of the times, Thakuri's father invested his inherited talent in farming and in coaching his two able sons from his deceased first wife in the science of proper behaviour, and thus he managed virtually to stop the inflow of emotions in their mental make-up. When his young second wife also died, leaving behind a baby, in order to express his deep love for his departed wife the father decided to turn the child into an expert in the field of faultless behaviour and diplomacy. But the herculean labour expended was obviously wasted – apparently fate decreed otherwise. Perhaps the mother, having taken shelter in heaven away from the pragmatic behavioural science of her husband, had decided to protect her child and started raining emotion on her son. Or, observing the possibility of another expert like himself, Kantilya, the ancient diplomat now abiding in heaven, might have decided to stultify the child's mind. Whatever the reason, the recalcitrant child did not even learn to distinguish between his own people and strangers, much less other advanced tenets. Disappointed, the father took leave of the world, placing this responsibility on his elder sons.

The elder stepbrothers were married and in charge of the household and fields, and the younger brother was given meals and clothes in exchange for his services. His poetic talent was useful to his brothers, since art does not allow worldly and especially practical wisdom to grow, and a man devoid of this wisdom might harm himself but certainly would not harm others.

When people in the community began commenting on the attitude of the elder brothers which had kept the younger one single, they married him to a well-behaved girl. As she entered the house the sisters-in-law began lecturing her on the virtues of service.

It would be irrelevant to say that the married couple could not be happy. When one slave becomes two, it is good for the owners but not for the slaves, for on one side the sovereignty increases but on the other slavery multiplies. Adopting the policy of alternately cajoling and punishing, the owners made their rule more secure by the expediency of dividing and ruling. But the slaves, owing to their helpless irritability and feeling of inferiority, would multiply one another's curses, and thus continue to obstruct the passage of their release.

If Thakuri and his wife had broken from the joint family and established their own household, then their services would not have been available. Therefore the sisters-in-law began to carry tales against the bride to her husband, representing her as a criminal. The husband's mind was tossed on the horns of belief and disbelief regarding his wife's culpability, but he did not console her by expressing faith in her innocence, nor did he resolve his doubts by declaring his suspicions.

The proud wife also did not speak up and instead expressed her annoyance through constant hard work. Thakuri, after all, was a poet, and dry reality could not pierce through the emotion-laden cloud of his imagination. If he got an opportunity to sing, he would not mind sitting on a perch the whole night guarding the field of the listener. If he found someone willing to listen to a recitation, he would not consider it below his dignity to prepare fodder for the listener's bullocks. He would go running for miles if someone wished to hear an epic. On the festival of Holi, while reciting poetry he would forget his thirst and hunger.

Because of his love for reciting poems he was unable to do any other work properly. And, unlike in the city, no one called him to sing an epic and then payed him fifty rupees, so Thakuri remained poor. A listener might express his generosity by tying a little sesame and jaggery in his scarf, or serve him sattu and chillies on a stone plate, or exhibit a love for poetry by baking two thick chappatis for him in the open fire. It is not true that Thakuri was not happy to receive these gifts. But he did not know that his love for reciting poetry had rendered him careless of his duties, and that this was the cause of his brothers' neglect, sisters-in-law's spite and wife's secret pain.

After a few years his wife gave birth to a daughter but, through lack of rest and nourishing food, the mother developed a fever. In due course, not receiving proper treatment, she got her release from this hard life, leaving behind an eighteen-month-old baby. Thakuri has returned late that night after reciting an epic in a nearby village. He had no memory of his mother's death and his old father's demise had not really touched him, but when his wife died in the first flush of youth, it broke his heart. The bitter tears succeeded in washing the make-believe world from his eyes. He became a real husband and father only after losing his wife.

Observing his daughter's neglect in the house, and imagining its effect on her health, he decided to live separately. Getting the property partitioned, he brought his mother's old sister to look after the household, but took care of the daughter himself. Bela, the daughter of the epic-loving father, would roam about on his shoulders and, when he worked in the fields, would supervise his work strapped to his shoulders. If someone laughed at this unconventional sight, Thakuri would say that if working mothers could work with babies, what was the shame in fathers doing the same. Besides, for Bela, he was father and mother.

When she grew to be seven years old, Thakuri brought home a well-behaved but orphaned nephew of a poetry-loving fellow caste member, and, having performed the engagement ceremony, began teaching his future son-in-law details of his work. Fate was probably against this country poet for when the bridegroom's education was completed smallpox gripped him. He somehow survived, but in his one eye the world became dark, and in the other so little light was left that the solid world looked like clouds of vapour to him.

The father desired to know the wishes of his daughter. But she was obstinate like her namesake, the heroine of the battle of Mahoba in the *Allah* epic, who wanted to be burned on a pyre of sandalwood in the garden of her father unless she could marry her chosen man. Bela did not want to shed her childhood friend, and so Thakuri was saved from the sin of breaking his promise.

Now the poet father-in-law had collected an interesting family – the mother's old sister, a blind son-in-law and a charming daughter. He taught his son-in-law tricks of versification. When Thakuri played his fiddle and sang, the son-in-law kept the beat on his tiny drum, and the old aunt, lost in reverie, would clang her tiny cymbals. In the movements of the working Bela, rhythm could also be discerned.

The household had a fat she-buffalo, two milch cows and a few acres of farm land, and these sufficed as a means of livelihood. The family came regularly to the annual bathing festival on the banks of the Ganges. Other pilgrims also flocked to the fair along with them.

Grandpa Thakuri is always willing to accept other pilgrims as his guests. However, in anchorage if one eats the grain of some one else he has to yield the religious virtue earned due to anchorage to the owner of the grain. That is why they all flock to the confluence with their own supply of foodstuffs tied in dirty bundles. But there is no harm in bartering grain for other food, even though there might be a great difference between the articles. One cannot resist smiling when observing the way these villagers effect a compromise between necessity and religious dictums. Offering a lump of jaggery, someone will obtain a pound of wheat flour, or will exchange four chillies for a pound of sweet potatoes, or barter a pint of yoghurt for a cupful of rice; in exchange for a spoonful of ghee, a tumblerful of milk is given to offer to the river Ganges.

Grandpa Thakuri really enjoys giving things away in these unequal barters, and he himself urges people to ask. This bartering goes on throughout the anchorage months. He is a sentimental person with a firm faith that everything will turn out for the best. As he picks up his fiddle and begins singing, gross materiality melts away before his vision. His kindness, affectionate attitude and emotionalism, once a common attribute of villagers, is now becoming rare. Village life is now so arduous and painful that there is not much scope for the development of humanity as such.

As in the past, this year the group around grandpa Thakuri is varied. Digging in the sand to form an improvised oven to cook meals is his daughter, lost in worldly cares. Stolidly seated, surrounded by fiddle, cymbals and a small drum, is the son-in-law, lost in day-dreaming. Puttering with ghee, an earthen pot and pumpkin, his aunt is busy solving the problems of this world and of heaven. All these constitute his own family. And the rest seem to be representatives of various groups and castes in this queer presidium.

There is an old widow who was queen of the household as long as her husband was alive. But now her nephews have disinherited and disenfranchised their childless aunt. She is treated like an aunt by Thakuri due to a village relationship, and he never forgets to bring her along to the confluence.

There is the wife of a grocer who, having deserted her for the daughter of a cooking-oil extractor,* now lives far away in the city of Calcutta. Wearing two silver toe rings as the double confirmation of her married status, and drawing the edge of her sari over her head up to her nose to maintain the social prestige of her husband's family, she now earns her livelihood by selling trinkets and spices. Every year she comes to the fair accompanied by her two adolescent sons. Suffering the arduous anchorage and standing in the waist-deep water of the Ganges, she prays to God that she will obtain the grocer as her consort in future lives. Even though her husband has ruined her present life, she is not willing to aspire to marriage with another man and forego the expected heavenly abode after death.

The third member is a widower belonging to the vegetable grower's caste. He manages his livelihood by sowing vegetables in the corner of someone else's field and by guarding the mango grove of a rich peasant. His wife had presented him with three daughters. Invariably the vegetable grower slept on an empty stomach after working very hard all day. After the birth of their fourth child there was only a little rice in the house and the eldest daughter boiled it in water. If the mother had eaten the rice, the children would have had to go to sleep hungry. She therefore strained the rice and drank the starchy water in which it had cooked, giving the rice to the

---

* An oil-extractor owns or operates a press used to extract cooking-oil from such seeds as mustard or sesame. The press is usually powered by a bullock walking round and round in a circle.

children. That very night she was gripped by high fever and on the third day the newly-born son and the mother both departed from this hard life.

Last year the vegetable grower fell from a tree, and now he cannot stand erect and is unfit for manual labour. The two adolescent daughters sometimes earn a little by making bullock dung into fuel cakes for the deserted wife of the grocer, or by plastering the Brahmin's house with cow dung, but the youngest girl has become a problem. Depending on the generosity of grandpa Thakuri the father comes each year with his three children to the anchorage, but what boon he asks from the Goddess Ganga is difficult to guess.

Fourth in the group is the Brahmin family. The pandit earns a meagre livelihood as the village priest and supplements this by narrating holy stories and solemnizing marriages. This is how he more or less solves the problem of earning a living. One knows not why God did not send some rich parishioner to release the priest from this grim poverty. By reading aloud hymns in praise of the holy Ganges, he tries to alter the dictates of his fate as written in the book of Chitra Gupta, the divine scribe.

The Brahmin's wife is basically a nice person, but her endless wait for a son has made her sour. She is not pleased with the worshipping activities of her husband, and in order to obstruct him she sometimes hides his piece of sandalwood in the grain container, hides his prayer beads away in a chink or locks up his holy books in a reed box.

When his widowed cousin died, the Brahmin was compelled to give shelter to an orphaned nephew. Since then, the boy has become a bone of contention. Instead of feeling consoled, the Brahmin's wife now suffers all the more from being childless. She grumbles that if the boy were of her own flesh and blood he would have been obedient and would have loved her. She does not understand that there is no sense in throwing such statements at an innocent child. The child has not even learned to distinguish those who are his own relations from those who are strangers, and he listens to her harangue with surprise. He is the same now as he was during his mother's lifetime, so why is his aunt getting so enraged? This question revolves in his mind and then he cries bitterly.

I passed a full month with these people and there are many memories, but one particular evening stands out.

I used to read until late at night, so my visitors would go out to sing their hymns elsewhere, with other anchorites. One day grandpa Thakuri respectfully suggested in an affectionate tone that it would be nice if the hymns were sung at least once at my cottage also. I keep away from noise, and it is not easy for me to join groups of hymn singers, but that day, perhaps out of curiosity, I accepted their invitation and a date was fixed.

It must have been three days before the full moon. In the morning a few flecks of cloud had gathered in the sky, but by evening these were washed away like a bevy of blue lotuses drifting off in the waves of evening to some unknown corner of the sky. After bathing in the Ganges and offering lighted earthen lamps to it, the people began gathering on the verandah of the hut, spilling over onto the sand outside.

On the verandah the pandit had planted a holy tulsi plant in a flower pot to worship, and had built up a platform of sand around it. On the sand platform Thakuri's aunt placed the copper image of Lord Krishna; the pandit put Lord Shaligram there, releasing him from the bondage of the tiny coloured wood container; Thakurani added an idol of Lord Shiva pulled out of a silver water pot; grandpa Thakuri brought his picture of Lord Ram, Sita and Hanuman, in a battered frame with broken glass; the blind man gave his bronze idol of the child Krishna with a sweet in his hand; the grocer's wife her mud idol of Lord Ganesh kept by her in remembrance of her absconded husband; altogether it looked as if the devotees had compelled their gods to assemble on the platform for a conference.

There was order in the seating arrangement also. On the verandah a mat was spread for me. On the right side the old ladies were seated, and slightly apart the grocer's wife and the Brahmin's wife sat. On the left was the row of children. To protect them from the cold, the grocer's wife had covered them with her cotton sheet. The pandit with his holy books was seated in front of the gods. A little away from him was grandpa Thakuri who was tuning his fiddle, and staying close to him in order to hear every line of the hymn clearly was the blind son-in-law who lovingly caressed his drum.

The shrivelled vegetable grower sat apart on the sand, wrapped
in a torn sheet. His back was bent, and it looked as if he were
trying to read something in the grains of sand. Other anchorites
had also joined the gathering. It was Bela's responsibility to bring
the incense, flowers and ghee for the ceremony, and she was
briskly shuffling about.

First the devotees sang a hymn in praise of the tulsi plant,
then the pandit completed the worship of the assembled gods and
goddesses. The holy Ganges water and tulsi leaves were then
distributed out of a bronze vessel by a tiny bronze ladle. Sprinkling
holy water over the assembly, in partly correct and partly incorrect
Sanskrit, the pandit recited verses in praise of the Ganges.
Then in a loud voice he recited that portion of Tulsidas' epic,
Ramayana, in which Lord Ram, his consort Sita and brother
Lakshman, ferry across the Ganges on the way to their exile
in the forest. Because most of the listeners remembered this
portion, they joined in with the pandit, thus helping to cover up
his out-of-tune vocalizations.

Finally, with a hymn in praise of Gouri and Ganesh, the
function began. Although none of them could be classed as good
singers, it must be accepted that the devotional intensity with
which they sang was really moving.

Poems of immortal poets like Kabir, Sur and Tulsi were sung,
and also couplets of unknown village poets. They had memorized
them all. One of them would lead with a couplet to be repeated
by the chorus voice of the assembly. The waves silently creeping
in to shore would ripple back as if keeping the beat.

There was sequence among the singers and variety according
to their ages. First two old ladies sang. The aunt of grandpa
Thakuri sang the hymn from the *Ramayana* where the brothers
Ram and Lakshman stood at the bank of the Ganges and
Lakshman called the boatman to bring his boat to their side
so they could cross the river, drawing a heart-rending picture
of the banished Lord Ram. A hymn in similar vein was sung by
Thakurani. These were sung haltingly due to the short-windedness
of the old devotees, but with such intense feeling that it seemed
the hymns were soaked with the passions of the heart which
weighed them down so they could not be sung continuously.
If in the pandit's wife's song, 'Mother, Baby Krishna is now

speaking,' there was a breadth of emotion, then in the song sung
by the grocer's wife, 'Krishna has left and men, women and cattle
all pine and cry for him on the banks of the river Yamuna,' there
was the depth of loneliness. In the songs of the vegetable grower,
'There is no way out except to tell the Lord,' and 'When the
heart is crossed with passion for the Lord there is nothing more
to say,' there was intense devotion. And in the song of the blind
young man, 'Let me not forget the memory of your vision, oh
Krishna,' there was devotional fervour.

After clearing his throat and closing his eyes, grandpa Thakuri
sang the following hymn:

The child Krishna is playing in the courtyard. He says his
mother is nice but his elder brother, Balram, is naughty. He does
not like meals, but eats only bread and butter. He does not like
to cover himself with a nice shawl, so his mother wraps him in a
black blanket. He will not go out and play with toys, but instead
demands a rough bamboo stick so he can bring the grazing cows
back to the barn.

Why the common people find so much of their own lives in the
life of Lord Krishna was shown to me that evening in ways that
are difficult to uncover otherwise. That voice, line and colour can
paint reality became evident to me in visualizing the images drawn
by their hymn singing. Everyone was caught up in the web of the
same emotion, the same heartbeat and intensity, from grownups
to children.

How long they continued singing I do not know, for when the
last piece was performed I woke up as if coming out of a trance.

Shortly afterwards, everyone was asleep on his bedding spread
out on the verandah, but inside my room, sitting in front of the
glow of the lamp, I was lost in thought.

The grocer's wife first peeped in from the outside and then,
stepping inside, said with great humility that I should please send
the lamp to her home, as her mother must be waiting for her—
meaning that I should extinguish the light and go to sleep.

A smile came to my lips, but I checked it. When their whole
world was anthropomorphic, why not imagine a mother waiting
for a lamp? I said, 'I will turn off the light.' She promptly snuffed
out the light by waving the edge of her sari. Obviously she was
afraid that I might do the job inappropriately by blowing it out,

which would be tantamount to murdering her by inviting in-auspiciousness to enter.

How long I sat there alone in the darkness I do not remember, but when I emerged from the room, the night was waning. The still moonlight, like a white silk sheet, was wrapped in the waves of the river and lying spread out over the sandy expanse. The two verandahs of my hut were suffused with the moonlight and as I looked at the people who were sleeping on the cold earth, or on sheets or piles of rice-stalks, I wondered why their interior life was so at variance with their exterior state. Did their instinctive politeness, sensitivity and intuitiveness, as well as their hard work, count for nothing, that even opportunities to earn a liveli-hood came so rarely to them? A mere glimpse into the abundance of their hearts' feelings had led me to imagine many contradictory pictures.

My heart searched for a memory of a poetry symposium which was similar, but out of hundreds of such all-India functions I could not recall even one which had touched me so much. Decorated halls, duly garlanded chairman, all passed before my mind. Surrounding the chairman were the poets seated on the platform, deficient in both looks and values. One had travelled third class after having received a first class fare from the symposium organizers. Another was already in town, but in order to stay on a few more days he demanded a fat fee before he would recite his poetry, so that after meeting his travel and living expenses he could save money. One, in order to enlarge his audience, had demanded at least four times the normal fee charged by others because of his sonorous voice.

Whatever greatness they could not express by means of their fees, was visible in the apparel they wore. Someone's recently custom-tailored suit was looking less westernized with its red stains of chewed betel leaves. Another, lost in cigarette smoke, was trying to be a mystic by dressing in a flowing silk kurta. The upright, unkempt hair of some looked like a shiny black floor. The artificially induced curls of someone's silky long hair proclaimed the victory of man over god.

Some old-fashioned poets, having no faith in the audience, had taken drugs, as was clearly seen in their involuntarily closing eyes.

It seemed as if the audience facing them had congregated to measure their fashionableness and not their poetry.

Like witnesses being called in court, the names of the poets were announced on the microphone. They would stand in front of the microphone either smiling shyly or preening like pigeons. Singing in tenor or bass, or in the absence of these capabilities speaking in a nasal drone, they would present their poetry wrapped in these artifacts and turn their heads expecting approbatory exclamations.

But still the audience would refuse to be impressed. Someone would shout, 'Your voice is awful!' or, 'Use expressive gestures too!' or a mere, 'Sit down!' Or they would demand the recitation of some smutty poem in order to embarrass the women present in the audience.

But the poets are not willing to accept defeat. 'If you don't want to hear that poem, listen to this one, my latest – '; they are determined not to leave the microphone. No one is ready to withdraw from either side or to vary his determination to score over the others.

Sometimes this exercise goes on for hours, but not a moment of real communication arises between the poet and audience in which his feelings reverberate in the hearts of the audience, and in which, leaving exhibitions aside, both could enjoy the insights of poetry. What can the poet say when the emotions embedded in his poem fail to touch the hearts of the audience, or the varied amorphous emotions of the audience fail to take on the structure of the theme of the poem?

When the function is over, the despondent audience and tired poets return to their homes. How little such symposiums have of ennobling influence on the participants can be easily seen by the fact that many amongst them do not mind going to professional singing prostitutes to while away their time listening to the music.

Emotions, when they fail to wash away man's pettiness, evil designs and distortions, become instead an instrument of his weaknesses. That is why affection and pity can contribute towards strength of character, and envy and anger toward its weakness. The village society seems able to submerge its individual weaknesses and differences of opinion in the ethos of group emotional expressions, and thus its members come out of the experience healthier.

Our culture-proud society has really shallow tastes in poetry, and
its aim is the attainment of cheap entertainment; the people who
participate try to tear each other down and thus enhance themselves.
In the village congregation, even feelings of high and low status are
unfrozen in the warmth of the group's sharing. The other is like a
wrestling arena, where, because of infighting, an intense rivalry
prevails.

I knew the triviality of these poetry symposiums, but their
emotional dross became clear to me only on that night. After a few
years, the conditions became so miserable that I stopped participating altogether, although it is really difficult for a poet struggling
to become known to create such a hiatus between himself and his
readers. Perhaps if this glimpse into the pious life of those villagers
had not led me to see artificiality so vividly, my reaction would
have been less violent. It becomes especially difficult when along
with a big event one is offered money, too, for wealth is the
controlling factor of this age.

No one now enquires about the tastes and qualifications of his
audience; if he is offered the desired sum, shaking off all principles,
he is willing to dance attendance to their whims. He is really a slave
to the wishes of his paymasters.

The poverty-stricken society which turned me into a non-believer
in such functions has not even been thanked by me.

When, after bathing on Basant Panchmi Day, grandpa Thakuri
and his friends left for their village, for the first time in my life I
missed the sound of peoples' voices. Since that time, I have seen him
again during such annual fairs. Many a time he has organized
hymn-singing on a boat or on the banks of the river Ganges, and has
served me kichri and pua while he narrated his life story to me.

I have seldom known a kinder man than grandpa Thakuri. Often
I have wondered about how he would have reacted and behaved in
our society, but I know it is difficult to erase the differences between
the two. Their outward life is lean and our inner life is empty. In
their society, deficiencies are in individuals and good motivations
exist in the society; against this, our weaknesses are social and our
strength is in individuals.

Grandpa Thakuri is the representative of his society and, as such,
his kindness, instead of becoming an individual oddity, genuinely
reflects the generally sympathetic social mores of village life. In

our society, if he were a weak person he would have been like the rest, and if he had strength of character he would have been an exception.

For the last two years he has not come to the fair. Sometimes I think about going to Saidpur to trace him in his village thirty-three miles away. I have noted down some of his hymn compositions and I intend to publish them with other folk songs. If I could find him, this collection would be still better.

Sometimes doubt arises in me – suppose he is no more? But I suppress this anxiety, asking myself how a man like Thakuri could really leave this world.

The last time he came he looked somewhat feeble. His hands held the fiddle firmly, but his fingers shook along with the strings. His feet were set steadily on the earth, but his knees trembled when he walked. His voice was still sweet, but a cough made it discordant. His eyes still looked at you with affection, but time had dimmed their light. His face was still radiant with laughter, but the skin around his lips had puckered. He had lost a few teeth, too. How helpless man is before time. His body has to pay dearly for the inevitable acknowledgement of its passage.

When he met me last, his aunt was already dead. How much he must have suffered from her enforced absence. He felt close to people he came in touch with only once; what then can be said about her who lived with him for years? I would not be surprised if her absence had triggered another anxiety in him – his daughter Bela would one day have to suffer separation from him; how would she then manage her livelihood? But then, he seldom expressed his worries.

When I questioned him about his health he replied, 'Now my time for departure is near, queen daughter. What can one say of ripe fruit – it can fall at any time!'

Jokingly I said, 'How can you live in heaven, grandpa? There no one will understand your Kut-Pad and Ulat basia, nor listen to your epics. You would be unfit amidst the singers and dancers of heaven.'

He beamed with happiness and said, 'That I know, daughter. I will create so much noise that god will despatch me again to this earth. Then I will transplant paddy, dig trenches, play on a fiddle and recite to you the whole epic of *Allha Udal*. I do not want heaven, but in order to ask for a new body I will go there. This one which he made is now old and tired.' And then he began singing, 'When the soul is leaving, why does his abode, the body, weep?'

I could not again go to the banks for anchorage during the fair. It is possible that he may have gone to heaven to ask for a new body, but his love for earth was so true and his attachment to life so abiding that he could not have lived in heaven long. The singers of the *Athar Veda* called themselves 'sons of earth', and grandpa was like one of them. For him life was the gift of mother earth, poetry a feeling for its beauty, love the movement of its attraction and strength another name for its motivation. And with such a man, if he chooses to sacrifice the high tomes of salvation for the sake of a lovely flower growing amidst grass, it need not surprise us.

Writing the story of grandpa Thakuri, the night has passed away and the dim rays of pre-dawn light breaking against the sky following the departure of the moonlight look like its shadow. Like the first invocatory couplet of some invisible nature poet, the chirping of the birds gradually reverberates through the silence. A breeze is blowing like the sighs of the newly awakened trees after their night slumber.

At this time, I suddenly remember a bygone morning. It appears to me as if grandpa Thakuri is seated on the banks of the river Ganges and is deeply engrossed in singing the morning melody, 'Wake up my Lord! The birds in the forest have begun twittering.'

Whom he now awakens by his morning melody is difficult to say.

Bibia

My washerwoman calls me 'elder sister', and her son Dhamrhi calls me 'auntie'.

The cultured section of our society might consider this to be impudence on the part of lowly workers, but I do not feel this is so, possibly because of my upbringing. In the village where my maternal grandparents lived I had to address the serf barber's old wife, Badamo, as 'grandma' and the old washerman, Nanku, as 'grandpa'. There, even those unfortunate serfs who performed the lowliest services had the right to be addressed as if they were relatives by the members of the landlord's family. That is why in such villages the urban relationship between money and respect was really not predominant.

The washerman, despite dissuasion, would persistently carry away my dress and other clothes and return them the next morning after washing them. The barber's wife would appear each day with oil and unguent and perform all the rituals of bathing me despite my crying and wilfulness. The dairy-maid would bring fresh butter and waste an hour or so trying to persuade me to eat a morsel. The gardener's wife, Rammo, would bring ornaments for me, fans woven of flowers, and the measure of the success of my education in the art of flower weaving can be seen now when my flower arrangements are so much admired.

Being the granddaughter of one family, it was as if I were related to the entire village community. They would not accept even a pittance for the services rendered to me. But then, of course, if

[86]

auntie dairy-maid Munia liked the new multi-coloured sari that my mother was wearing, getting hold of its edge she would harass my mother so much that she had then and there to undress and offer Munia the desired sari. The gardener's wife, auntie Rammo, would not agree to grind the myrtle which is used to decorate hands and feet on festive occasions unless and until she had obtained a pair of expensive studded shellacked bangles.

On the day the ritual of having my ears pierced occurred, or on a birthday or other such festive occasion, grandma Badamo would not begin dancing her community's traditional dance unless she had obtained from my grandmother her muslin skirt and specially embroidered scarf. That my grandfather's jacket had been removed from a peg in our living room and had adorned the body of grandpa Nanku would become known only when he returned with his new outfit splattered with coloured water after playing Holi in every nook and corner of the village. These relationships were not confined to certain individuals or generations, but were all-pervasive. This way of relating has been observed for generations and still continues.

If this childhood influence has not left me despite my present city life, I would only take it as natural, but how others came to divine it is a mystery to me.

For more than a decade I have not changed my servant, milkman, washerman or tonga driver. If there can be any reason for such a change except death, it is known neither to them nor me.

Dhamrhi's mother has been washing my clothes since my student days. She had the misfortune to lose her children one after the other so, in order to fool the hostile stars, she put her newborn son in a cane winnowing basket and sold him to a neighbour for one dhamrhi. After the sixth day she bought him back for five dhamrhis, and to commemorate the sale and purchase she named him Dhamrhi Lal. You can attribute it to the folly of the creator or the strength of Dhamrhi – in any case he managed to avoid the valley of death. Dhamrhi is now grown up and married, but he still has not stopped his childish pranks. Sitting arrogantly in the courtyard of our house he will shout to Bhaktin who is working in the kitchen, 'Mother Bhaktin! I know how to drink tea, too. If you have brewed some for auntie, give me a cupful!'

At this, Bhaktin's round nostrils dilate, her brow furrows, the lines of her forehead draw closer together and the wrinkles around her lips contort. But she does give him tea. Yes, it is true that she offers him tea in a tumbler whose nickel polish has worn off, revealing the bronze beneath. Even then he will not leave her in peace. Solicitously he will say, 'Isn't auntie having a snack? By God, ma'am, tea brewed by you is so sweet that I can drink it without sugar, there is so much sweetness in your hands. This time I will wash your sari so white that it will rival the feathers of a duck.'

It becomes difficult not to laugh at this gentleman seated on a bundle of dirty clothes in the courtyard, drinking tea brewed by Bhaktin from a worn metal tumbler.

To earn more money, mother and son take away even my clean clothes to be washed. On being told a towel has been taken out only that morning, the son will reply, 'One end is muddy now, and I need to tie fried gram in the other end.' When I tell them I have worn a sari only briefly, the mother inquires, 'Would it be wrong if I also wore it for a day, sister?' Now what can auntie do? Dhamrhi needs the towel to tie fried gram in and his mother wants to wear the clean sari – but the washing charges have to be paid by the auntie.

I should protest against this injustice, but the silhouettes of two memories, which are etched on my mind, suddenly stop me from speaking out. The passage of time has dimmed their outlines, but the pervasiveness of their sadness has neither faded nor been washed away.

Sometimes, on seeing a person, picture or scene, the mind flashes back to a contrasting scene, picture or person. Observing this pair of laughing mother and son, the memory of Bibia and her mother knocks at my mind.

Bibia's mother never told me anything about herself, but the helplessness in her visage, the signs of injuries on her hands, the unnatural lameness of her legs – all these were clear indicators of her hard life. Perhaps she had grown so used to the torture of her quarrelsome drunkard husband that in its absence she would no longer want to live in this world.

When her parents died, Bibia's condition became somewhat difficult, for now only her elder brother, Kanhai, his wife and a grandmother were left in the family. Being old, the grandmother would sometimes dub a mistake of the granddaughter as unpardonable, while at other times the same mistake was of no consequence. There was the traditional animosity between the sister-in-law and Bibia, and since several brothers and sisters had died between the birth of the eldest brother, Kanhai, and the youngest child, Bibia, the age difference between them was so great that they could not become companions to each other.

Perhaps Bibia used to come to me now and then to hear a few words of sympathy. Her mother had called me 'elder sister', and to follow the same relationship Bibia began calling me 'auntie'.

Generally washerwomen have dark complexions and well rounded faces. Bibia had the charm of a rounded face along with a beautiful brown complexion. And her pleasant behaviour was an added attraction. She was always laughing, showing her white teeth. Her big eyes were lively and restless, as if observing everything around her. With her well-proportioned figure, Bibia would not be taken for a washerwoman, but she was only that and the most unfortunate among them.

The lassitude and delicacy which is normally associated with such beauty was totally absent in Bibia. As a matter of fact, it was difficult to find a person as hard working as she was. She enjoyed doing not only her own chores but also a share of the work of others. Snatching the broom from her grandmother's hands, she would sweep the courtyard and the entire house; snatching the dough from her sister-in-law she would sit down in the kitchen to bake chappatis; taking the heavy coal-filled iron out of her brother's hands she would begin ironing the clothes. She worked harder than anyone while applying saltpetre to the dirty clothes before boiling them, or in drying the washed clothes, or carrying the stacks of clean clothing to the customers.

But she was very proud. She liked wearing fine clothes, a desire she fulfilled by wearing the customers' apparel. Her mother had left a bit of jewellery which she wore with delight.

Her engagement was fixed even before her birth and in her fifth year the marriage was solemnized but, before she could go to the husband's place for consummation of the marriage, the death of the bridegroom frustrated the efforts of her well-wishers to unite the couple. Under these circumstances it is considered sinful for a widow from a higher caste to marry again, but in lower castes it is looked upon as a social crime if the widow does not remarry.

Kanhai used to live in a village across the river Yamuna, but he searched in the city for a washerman for his sister. On an auspicious day the substitute bridegroom reached the village of his prospective in-laws, accompanied by his relatives. Meat was cooked in a large cauldron and puris were fried in a big iron frying pan. Several bottles of country liquor had also been obtained. The bride's and bridegroom's people danced, drank and feasted until late in the night, and the festivities stopped only when they had all floundered on the floor dead drunk.

I did not see Bibia for several months after that and I thought she must be busy settling down in her new household.

After several months, she suddenly appeared before me one day. Dressed in dirty, tattered clothes, her body looked anaemic. Her cheeks had blotches of shadowy patches. There were neither tears of sadness in her eyes nor a smile of happiness on her lips. In her expression was neither acceptance of guilt nor demand for justice for an innocent. Only a wordless indifference emanated from every gesture.

What words she uttered conveyed the sense that from now on she planned to wash my clothes and would cook her meals separately on the verandah of her brother's house. Gradually it emerged that her husband had thrown her out of the house. He had said that there was no place for such a woman in his house and that she could either pass her days with her brother or take another man.

Obviously she must have been turned out for her lack of fidelity – this doubt naturally arose in me. But when I questioned her it pierced her shield of indifference and she burst out crying. ' Now you also believe this, auntie! Mother has gone to heaven – now what will I do with my life?'

Her sorrow made me feel repentant, but when I heard the full story from her grandmother I was indeed annoyed with myself. Bibia had tried hard to organize her husband's household, but Ramai was an inveterate gambler and drunkard. This trait is common among washermen and drunkenness is considered nothing unusual.

On the first day itself, Ramai returned late in the night dead drunk. Since there was no other woman in the house, newly-arrived Bibia had carefully cooked a meal, boiling lentils and frying vegetables, and she was waiting for him with the dough ready to bake hot chappatis. As Ramai entered reeling, seeing her there he began hurling so many filthy and smutty epithets at her that she lost her self control. As it is she was short-tempered, and these insults were heaped on her in her own house by her own husband. Enraged, she spoke out, 'Aren't you ashamed of yourself? Talking to your wife as if you had come to a prostitute – shame on you.'

Despite his intoxication the husband felt insulted. Baring his teeth and glowering he sneered, 'Married! You've already swallowed one husband and have come to the second – maybe to become another chaste wife like Sita? How lucky for me – I touch your feet in respect.'

Unable to restrain herself, Bibia picked up the steel tongs and threw them at him. Trying to protect himself from this flying missile he precipitately fell on his face and, entering the dark room, the wife locked herself in. In the morning, opening the door as she emerged, she saw the husband had already gone off somewhere.

Such incidents continued thereafter every day. In addition to drinking, he was also fond of gambling, which is worse. After his intoxication leaves him, a drunkard may become a human being, but a gambler is never in his right mind.

Ramai's gambling friends came from a wide variety of castes and the articles with which they gambled were also varied – clothes, shoes, money, utensils, anything at hand. One would win the necklace of someone else's wife, and another the nose ring of someone's daughter-in-law. One would lose his sister's arm bracelet, and someone else his granddaughter's bangles. In brief, before coming to the den there was a necessity for some robbery, too.

One day Ramai's gambler friend, Karim, glowering with his bloodshot eyes, said, 'Friend, you've got a nice piece there – why not put her up for betting? If you're lucky, you might win a heap of rupees and small coins – a heap.'

Everyone wholeheartedly supported this suggestion. Ramai felt the urge to gamble away his wife, but either he remembered the tongs or a burning log of wood – he somehow stopped himself. Offering an excuse he said, 'Today I have the cash. The wife is meant for some other day when I don't have money.'

It did not take long for this news to reach Bibia. For such a proud woman this was like putting a spark to a heap of hay. Unfortunately, a few days later she found Karim loitering in front of her house. Immediately taking out the long knife used for cutting vegetables, knitting her eyebrows she threatened that if Ramai did anything of the kind she would rip open both their bellies with that very knife. No matter what punishment would be meted out to her later, she would certainly do it. She wasn't a cow or calf that one could sell to a butcher or give away to a priest so he could ford the Vaitharni River and reach heaven.

Karim was stunned, but the next day in front of his gambler friends he said to Ramai, 'What is this? Such an evil-eyed woman in a decent man's house. She threatens people with a knife on the flimsiest pretext like a crazy person. Someday she will attack you, too. Be careful, friend, you are flirting with death by staying in that house.'

The cowherd, Lakhna, repeatedly nodding his head, spoke in a serious tone, 'These days women are out to beat up men. It certainly looks as if Kalyug, the immoral age, is now showing its fangs.' Mahgu exhibited his knowledge of the sacred Shastras. 'On the other hand, look at the behaviour of Lord Ram's consort, Sita. He sent her into exile, but she never complained and contentedly spent her days in the jungle with her children.' Khelawan supported Mahgu, 'Sita was a virtuous woman. When challenged, mother earth opened her womb to absorb her. You can't expect a wife like yours to be genuinely virtuous.'

Poor Ramai could give no reply. That his wife could not be counted among the virtuous women was shameful for him. He could perhaps live with this shame and sorrow, but it was very difficult to live day and night under the shadow of fear. A woman who was not afraid to brandish a knife – would she be afraid to use it? Poor Ramai really grew so fearful that he began avoiding even the shadow of his wife. Some time passed like this, but in the end Ramai unambiguously conveyed the message that he would not keep Bibia in his house. The village tribunal also supported him, since its members were victims of the same habits. If they had wives like Bibia to whom they could not go after drinking or gambling, they would also have to shed their habits.

Finding no way out, Bibia returned home and started living as in the past. It would be wrong to say that her sister-in-law's taunts did not hurt her, but she could still cling to her grandmother and cry on her shoulder. She did four times more work than before, leaving her bed before anyone else was awake and going to sleep only after everyone else had retired. She would put on neither fine clothes nor ornaments and would not participate in singing or dancing. She was heartbroken because of the insults of her husband, and the calumny of the community was making it even harder for her to live. Because it could not be easy to turn away such a pretty and hardworking wife, everyone therefore concluded that she must have some serious moral infirmity.

Her brother Kanhai once again tried to get her settled. This time he selected an elderly widower and father of four children from a nearby village.

But Bibia vociferously objected to this. She did not eat for several days and cried for hours, 'Brother I will not go. I will break my head against the wall, but I will not leave the house of my parents.' She tried to persuade her brother thus, but all her efforts were futile. Her brother was of the view that maintaining his young sister in the house was an invitation to trouble. If she ever digressed from virtue, he would be socially ostracized by the community. And he didn't have enough money to pacify the community tribunal by offering a feast and thereby becoming socially acceptable again.

At last Bibia's consent was expressed through her apathy. Someone dressed her in a light red bridal sari, another made up her eyes, and someone else fitted her wrists and ankles with the jewellery of the bridegroom's deceased wife. That is how she once again went off to new in-laws.

When I did not receive any news of her for a full year, I felt relieved, supposing that the wild girl must by then have been tamed.

Not only me, but her brother, sister-in-law, grandmother and other relatives also were feeling relieved. Then suddenly one day news came that she had returned to her brother's place again, and with more calumny. This time she did not come to anyone to ask for anything. It was reported that she neither did any household chores nor left her room. In the same dark room of the house where hay for the burro and heaps of coal for fuel were stored, she would either sit or just lie there with her face covered. With persistent persuasion she would eat a few mouthfuls of food, otherwise she was not interested in eating either.

Hearing all of this I naturally became concerned. A speck of doubt rising from some unknown corner of my heart was slowly dislodging my faith in her. Was Bibia really a woman of bad character? If not, why was she unable to carve a respectable niche for herself in any household? Girls far less beautiful than she have been able to build a world for themselves. What infirmity did this unfortunate girl have that she could not even live with her husband?

Amidst these ruminations, one day her grandmother arrived and, repeatedly wiping the tears from her dim eyes with the torn edge of her sari, she narrated to me the story of her granddaughter's misfortune.

Two previous wives of Bibia's husband had already died. The first wife had left a son in her memory who, if not equal in age to his stepmother, might be older by four to six months. The second wife had left three daughters; the eldest was nine and the youngest three years old.

Jhanku had married the third time only to acquire a governess for his children. If he had any love for his new wife, it was not noticeable in his behaviour. In the early morning he would tie up his bundle of dirty clothes and chappatis, and would go to the river bank, returning in the evening. Taking the bundle off the back of his burro and releasing the animal to graze, he would again go out and never return before midnight.

It was rumoured that most of his spare time was spent in the company of a particular low-caste woman. Different views were held regarding their intimacy. Because they belonged to different castes, he had not been able to enter into any permanent ties with that family, and had escaped from the wrath of the community tribunal only because of his amiable nature and blameless wives.

The husband of that woman had become a groom for some rich family in the city, but his wife suddenly developed so much affection for the house of her in-laws that she considered that leaving it would be the height of sacrilege.

If a woman was not needed for himself, Jhanku still needed a fellow caste-woman who could look after the children, but no washerwoman had mustered up the courage to become his wife. Bibia's plight in the community was different, however. She was so up to her neck in the ocean of calumny that even Jhanku's proposal came to her like a rescue ship.

In this way, without involving his heart, he managed to bring in Bibia as his wife. It is true he did not harass her in any way. He did not even ask that she come to the river bank to do washing. So her household skill was being tried only in grinding, cooking and looking after the children. Whether she was happy or unhappy with this respectful but indifferent response from her husband no one ever knew, for by devoting herself heart and soul to the household and children she had blocked the way for any other emotion.

She was preoccupied with chores from morning until midnight. Then with the two younger daughters, making one lie on her left and the other on her right as she stretched out on the broken cot, she would soar away from the worries of the world. With the dawn, the next page of the old book of duty was already open.

Their mud house had only two rooms whose doors opened toward the outside verandah. The doorway between the rooms was frameless. Before going out, Jhanku would close the door of one room and put a padlock on the latch, so that when he returned late in the night no one was disturbed.

Bibia would set aside baked chappatis for her husband and then go to sleep. If he returned hungry he would eat them, otherwise he would take them with him to the river bank in the morning.

Deprived of her husband's love, she filled her empty heart with the innocent affection of her step-children. With utter love and care she would bathe them, groom their hair, feed them and put them to sleep. Persons who did not know assumed she was their real mother, and an extremely affectionate one.

Seeing the way she was bringing up the children, Jhanku grew complacent about the household. He concerned himself more with keeping the storage containers filled with grain than with his wife's barren life.

This also would not have been bad, if his eldest son had not returned home from his grandparents' place. Due to the absence of a mother and the indifference of the father he had become a vagabond. Unlike the other members of his community, he liked to apply scented oil to his body, and kept cotton wool dipped in cologne in the hollow of his ear, roaming around with his fighting partridge and wrestling.

A washerman who drinks and gambles is not considered to have transgressed the definition of a gentleman, but laziness is unacceptable. In the work he undertakes for a livelihood there is no scope for laziness or cheating. A labourer can escape undetected even if he wastes some time during the work day or does a bad job occasionally but a washerman is unable to do so.

He has to return the correct number of clothes to the customer, put in the required effort getting them clean, and keep in mind the extent to which each cloth can tolerate ironing and starch. If he began wasting the required time for these tasks, he would not be able to wash four loads in a month and the problem of earning a livelihood would become acute. Probably for this reason, devotion to work is commonly found in both the good and bad washerman. There can be a variation in extent, but total absence is an exception.

Jhanku's son, Bhikhan, was such an exception. With some persuasion the father had got him married to the daughter of a poor washerwoman but, seeing no improvement in her son-in-law, she found a hard-working husband for her daughter and completed the consummation ceremony with a new bridegroom instead. So Bhikhan could not set up his own home, much less become a decent householder. The father was himself in no position to offer counsel to his son. but, ultimately tiring of the boy's escapades, he punished him by banishment from the house.

This is how it came about that, at the time his stepmother entered his father's house, he was busy gaining expertise in flying kites and arranging partridge fights at his maternal grandparents' home. The father did not send for him but the presence of the stepmother made him eager to return.

One day, adorning himself with a loose shirt of striped cloth and wearing a loin cloth with a fine border, he assiduously groomed his curly hair. Then, holding the partridge cage in one hand and a bundle of fried rice for his half-sisters in another, he arrived at the door of the house. The father was not home, but the stepmother left nothing undone in welcoming her stepson. Mixing treacle in a tumblerful of water, she offered him the beverage. She baked eggplant for his meal along with the lentil curry and, putting a bed in the other room, she made arrangements for him to rest.

The confrontation between the father and son did not turn out to be an affectionate reunion, for on one side there was the anxiety of the unknown, and on the other side a determined disobedience. Jhanku clearly told him that if did not behave like a gentleman he would immediately be turned out of the house. Bhikhan, pouting and squinting his eyes, turned his face away in disdain as he listened to his father's exhortation, but he said nothing which would indicate that he agreed to behave like a decent man.

To the extent that a man without character doubts everyone else, to that same extent a man with character will not. Jhanku now willingly undertook to carry the burdensome load of protecting the wife for whom he previously had not undergone one moment of anxiety.

He would return home on time, keep a sharp eye on his son, and search for any change in the behaviour of his wife. But the son, disregarding his father's watchful eye, would hover around his stepmother. When she would squat to clean the pots, he would feed his partridge near her. When she would go out to dry washed clothes, he would sit naked and apply oil to his muscular thighs and arms. As she returned with a pitcher of water from the well, hiding behind the trunk of the shady mahua tree he would sing a smutty song, 'Fair damsel, walk slowly lest the water in your vessel spill over.'

One day, while eating, his attempts at endearment reached such an extent that pulling a burning stick out of the oven the stepmother threatened him saying, 'I'm your father's wife. If I hear such talk again I will beat your skin off.' At this ennobling response of his stepmother, instead of feeling ashamed he became angry. Such men are very proud of their skill in seduction, and if they fail to influence a particular woman it hurts their ego so badly that they do not hesitate to wreak vengeance. As a result of the stepmother's sermon, and with no other cause, Bhikhan began nursing thoughts of malice toward her.

Bibia, despite not being quite happy with the behaviour of her husband, was not annoyed with him. A proud person usually accepts respectful treatment even when it is meted out unemotionally but rejects abundant love which is offered with disdain. Jhanku had no love for his wife, but like other washermen he showed her no disrespect. This behaviour was more valuable in the eyes of a woman like Bibia than love, and she was grateful with every pore of her body. And if cruel fate had not mockingly sent the stepson she would contentedly have passed the rest of her life in that house. But even this happiness slipped away from her.

She now noticed such a show of pretended intimacy in the behaviour of Bhikhan that she grew apprehensive. In order not to disturb the peace of the family, she did not complain to her husband, but she failed to foresee the cruel outcome of her silence.

Whenever her name was mentioned in front of others, the son would put on a show of lascivious shyness and deep attachment, and his friends began spreading rumours about their relationship. In their homes, other washerwomen made comment to their husbands about the depravity of Bibia's deception, and when praising their own faithfulness would ask for necklaces and bangles from their husbands as certificates of their loyalty. On the bank of the river, within earshot of Jhanku, the washermen would seek to demonstrate their knowingness about the woman's frailty.

It was not surprising, therefore, that hearing these intimations of the misbehaviour of his wife and his own cowardice, his patience reached breaking point. One day when he was returning, deeply hurt, from the river bank, his son met him on the way. Not caring for anything, Jhanku began beating his son with the stick which he used to prod his burro. Pretending to be repentant, the son laid all the blame on his stepmother and wept at his helpless degradation. This is how Bhikhan executed his strategy of revenge.

If he wished, Jhanku could have demanded an explanation from his wife, but he had observed such clear proofs of her guilt that he did not think it necessary to observe this formality. Bibia had not even once obstinately demanded jewellery or clothes; not once had she challenged the woman who was the recipient of his favours; and she had never sulked about his indifference. These actions would have proved her affection for the husband; those who had no attachment were naturally indifferent. And then, people consider it logical that such an uninvolved person should be interested in someone else. According to this infallible logic, giving an opportunity for an alibi to a person whose guilt is proven would be like rewarding the accused. For her, the best warning would be meting out punishment.

That night, for the first time, Bibia was beaten. Fists, slaps, kicks and sticks were freely used as convenient, but the accused neither admitted her guilt nor begged forgiveness, and she never cried. If inclined, Bibia was quite capable of responding to kicks and fists with rolling pin and tongs, but she had developed so much respect for Jhanku that she would not raise her hand against him.

The wife's silence was taken as a confession of guilt by her husband, and when he grew tired of beating her he pushed her out into the verandah and, closing the doors from inside, lay on his bed gasping for breath.

In remembrance of the heavy beating with fists, her body developed several swollen bruises, blue lines could be seen on her skin recording the times the sticks fell on her, and her joints were painful because of the kicks. Besides that, the door closed from inside told her that she would never be forgiven. Stumbling, crying and sighing in the darkness on the narrow, seemingly fated footpath, she began walking to her parents' village.

No member of the community tribunal had appeared to teach Jhanku the duties of a husband, but in order to punish Bibia for her alleged straying from the path of duty, the tribunal held its meeting. Bhikhan begged forgiveness, narrating the false story of the allurements offered by the stepmother and his own innocent weakness. Any deficiencies on the path to forgiveness were filled by his maternal uncle and grandmother with the offer of money.

Men are so attracted to the weaknesses of others that they are willing to accept as true the words of men without character in order to discover infirmities in upright people. Just as a thief has no use for honesty, if a man is bereft of any good qualities and has no faith in the cultivation of such traits, he will naturally not believe another person could be equipped with these. The false ideas of such men are accepted as true in society, and numerous excavators of guilt are found among persons with infirmities themselves.

No one had any illusions about Bhikhan's character, but in order to find fault with Bibia it became necessary to accept his confession of guilt. She could not come to offer proof of her innocence; if she had arrived, the fate of the members of the tribunal at the hands of the angry lioness can easily be imagined.

Bibia's grandmother had died, but the brother could not banish his eternally unhappy sister from his house, so he was ostracized by the community.

In the meantime, because of fever, I had to go to the hills to recuperate. When my health improved, I returned and made inquiries about Bibia. I was informed that she had gone away and no one knew where; the brother who was defamed due to the misdemeanour of his sister had taken refuge with his father-in-law in another town. No one knew if Kanhai was sad at having shaken off his sister, but everyone knew that thanks to the influence of his father-in-law, who was head of his community, he had regained the happiness of being acceptable to the community.

The community of washermen in the village were not unanimous in their assessment of Bibia. Some held that she was guilty and judged her harshly, but a few considered that her false steps had been ordained by fate, and took a more charitable view. An old woman told me that Bibia had become distraught at her brother's ostracization. He had been asked to spend two hundred rupees to be taken into the community again, a sum that Kanhai could never have collected even if he worked for it his entire life. During these days of adversity a first son was born to Kanhai. His wife was not happy with Bibia, as it was. And now she would loudly bemoan their bad luck and express irritation at the stupidity of her husband, 'Is it due to our own bad luck that our first born son is to be neglected socially? We have done nothing wrong, but still the people of the community won't come to feast at our house. My household is ruined because of someone else's sin. A wise person would die and leave us in peace.'

Listening to these suggestive undertones, one day Bibia just disappeared.

Everyone had a firm belief in her lack of virtue, and such a disappearance was also taken as proof of her moral infirmity. She was not a virtuous wife, so what else could she do but run away with someone? If she had wanted to commit suicide she would have drowned herself when her husband expelled her, or hanged herself in someone else's house immediately after returning to her brother's home. It was not logical that she would decide to take her life after she had ruined his family.

It is always difficult to fathom a woman's mind, but if she has a unique personality no man can really understand her behaviour.

Although there was no known proof of Bibia's intimacy with any man of the village, several inferences based on guesses were construed as true. Clearly, without anyone's knowledge, Bibia must have found a companion for her unknown journey.

Many days later, when I went to the village to give medicines to an old, sick man, some light was thrown on her mysterious journey. He told me that two days before she had disappeared she had asked him to bring her a half bottle of country liquor. She had no cash, and took off the silver earrings given to her by her mother and put them in his palm. Among the washerwomen, she was the only one not addicted to drinking, and the man was surprised at her request. On being questioned, she replied that her brother wanted to give his family a feast at the ceremony of name-giving for her nephew, but if he came to know of the liquor in advance he would finish it off, so it was necessary to obtain it secretly.

Next day, when he brought her the half bottle wrapped in a dirty cloth and wanted to return the change, closing his palm she calmly said it would be better if he kept the money himself for the time being; she would ask for it if she required it.

Several girls playing on the outskirts of the village remember seeing her walking hesitatingly toward the river with a small bundle wrapped in dirty cloth. A shepherd boy had also seen her in the evening, repeatedly drinking something from her cupped hand and then cleaning her mouth with the dirty water of the river and laughing like a maniac.

At this, a doubt began to disturb me. No one would make arrangements for an intoxicating drink before undertaking a journey. Or if it were needed, why could not the alleged companion, in whose existence the village had full faith, have obtained it? What was the pressing necessity which made Bibia sell the last heirloom of her mother in order to possess it? And did she have so much money to take with her that she left behind even the change from the liquor purchase?

In August, when the heaving Yamuna river flows with lashing strength against its banks, no one goes there to wash clothes. Due to the kindness of the rains, tiny ponds and rivulets become filled with water and the washermen do their washing in this water. Then why had only Bibia gone there? Arguing like this, I reached a conclusion which disturbed me.

Suicide is the acceptance by a man that he has lost in the battle of life. A person like Bibia can never accept defeat, even after losing the battle, but who can say that she may not have planned all this to forget her last defeat. The world had banished her; accepting this and spreading the edge of her sari in supplication, could she have sought a niche in the thundering waves?

I know of a daughter-in-law belonging to a respectable family who, on being derided for childlessness, had stood up to her knees the whole night in the water of the river Yamuna; in the early morning an old man who had come to bathe escorted her back to the family. She told me that it was not love for life that had shaken her resolve to die but that the idea of the victory exclamation by others; 'She couldn't do anything, so she took her life,' had para-lysed her feet and she could not proceed toward deep water.

In Bibia was an inextinguishable spark of revolt. The world had insulted her and she was running away without challenging it – the mere thought of this, like a storm shredding clouds that have not yet released their rain, would have shattered her determination to commit suicide. But she had already lost all her weapons to wage battle and even a man with vast courage, when not in his senses, can run away from battle and be dubbed a coward.

The reason inferred by the world for her disappearance suits its system of logic, but I am not bound to accept it.

Even now, whenever my boat attempts to cross the thundering Yamuna which is madly trying to imitate the ocean, the story of Bibia knocks at my memory. One day, beneath the dark nimbus clouds, throwing away her oars she had released her boat of life.

On which unknown bank the dilapidated boat of that lonely person finally succeeded in docking cannot be told.

The Mute Woman

Although I try to avoid writing letters on my own behalf, writing letters on behalf of others has become almost my ordained duty. In the countryside or in the hill villages, I have to discharge the functions of a professional scribe.

Somewhere a disconsolate mother is anxious to convey her motherly affection to the son who has run off to some far away place; or a daughter-in-law who is confined by the four walls of her husband's house wishes to remind her brother to come during the rainy season and take her home to their mother. Sometimes a deserted, lonely wife wants to tell her husband who is living in some distant place with another woman that he should at least write to her about his welfare. A sick person, invoking brotherly affection, wants to compel a brother labourer living in the city to send him money. On the basis of blood relationship, an uncle wants his nephew to send him money to buy bullocks for ploughing. A brother-in-law writes to his wife's brother reminding him of their marriage relationship and beseeching him to redeem his mortgaged fields.

Thus, there are widely divergent groups among the letter writers. The subjects of the letters are so varied that even an expert letter writer would become stumped, and my own skill in letter writing is even less than that as a rhymer of verses. Coupled with my absolute lack of skill, the inability of the letter senders to state clearly what they wish to convey makes the letter writing even more difficult.

[103]

They gush out emotions with neither sequence in their sentences nor clarity in their ideas. If they are interrupted, they think that the writer lacks ability and that nothing good will come of the letter.

To put sequence in the story from their disorderly and involved language, to juxtapose this with their confused and indistinct ideas, and then to give all this the form of a letter is obviously not simple.

There is further difficulty in putting the facts in the letter in modern form, for these villagers are not only specialists in the traditional way of letter writing, but they are also blind followers in the method.

At the top of every letter it is necessary to write, 'Blessed is Lord Ganesh,' or 'Oh, Lord Ram!' Without this preface the letter is not accepted as valid. The persons to whom the letters are addressed, even though they might be deep in poverty and extremely ugly, must still be addressed as 'Prosperous and Incomparable One'.

There are no fewer traps set for the substitute writer in the subject matter of the letter, also, since in order to understand one story he gets involved in several sub-stories. The sender always wishes to narrate his own story along with these several sub-stories. Not only this, but the sequence of the incidents will be out of joint with the endless flow of the story, yet the sub-stories must be tied to the continuity of the main theme. If someone wants money from a relative he can only say so after the simultaneous narration of several incidents in his life, and he will be satisfied only after naming the rich village landlord and the lowliest resident of the village as witnesses to his penurious predicament.

These letter senders give such a lively description of several past events that the writer feels baffled. He is not allowed to decide for himself what he should include or leave out, and even if he took any such liberties while writing they would request him to read the letter to them, putting him under further difficulties. Whatever they wish to be written has been repeated orally so many times that they are immediately able to discern the portions left out by the writer.

You cannot get rid of the senders by saying that no space is left for writing more. Gazing with eyes of entreaty at the writer and pointing with their gnarled fingers to some blank corner of the letter, they so plaintively request that the left-out portion be written there that this cannot be ignored. To eliminate some portion of their message for the sake of leaving a margin or the corners of the letter blank is unjustified from their point of view. They stop only after the entire page has been smeared over with written words.

The problem of understanding their feelings is no less arduous. As you become able to grasp one facet of their feelings, you find yourself flooded with a myriad sentiments. These villagers are more sentimental than the intellectuals of the city, and because of this, every portion of the message serves as a catalyst for new emotional outbursts. As the story progresses, you will encounter in disorderly sequence their sense of humour, their pains, their wrath and their repentance. There will be glimpses of their absorbing affection, of depression due to neglect by dear ones, and sometimes expressions of philosophic resignation or talk about ethical behaviour. In brief, the feeling changes according to incident, time and place.

But it is not easy to know which of these numerous sentiments should be given prominence in the letters written on their behalf. A father will want to admonish his son, who lives far away, for his neglect and disregard of duties. The letter writer, while inscribing harsh words of admonition on his behalf, will suddenly feel the tearful pathos in those sentences. And as you raise your head, instead of a harsh, judge-like person you will find a weeping, sentimental, humble father in front of you. Since it is a problem even to identify which of the two facets is more true, to choose which of these to write down is far more difficult.

Many a time I have had to tear up the letter which was being written by me because the person dictating the letter ceased to be what he appeared to be at the beginning. Under such conditions it would have been not only unjust but also harmful from a practical point of view to send that letter, for after reading it, not understanding the sense behind the lines, the addressee would have formed wrong impressions.

Even after resolving all the problems of the letter sender, one hurdle still remains: in this one person's letter all the other villagers want to add something on their own behalf.

On one person's behalf a respectful salutation is to be expressed; then comes a shower of benedictions from another. Friendly greetings from someone, then an enthusiastic greeting from another.

Someone, by writing 'Letter writing is half meeting,' wishes to exhibit his poetic talent; then someone, wanting to write 'What is decreed by the Lord will happen,' wishes to display his philosophical nature. Someone else will consider it necessary to inform the addressee that he has sold a calf, and another relates that he has purchased a she-buffalo. It is imperative to advise the addressee that one man has been dispossessed of his fields and that the thatched roof of someone else's house has collapsed. One is keen to narrate the story of the deepening and cleaning of his well, and another tells of the drying-up of the pond.

Rarely can one find a man who does not want to send some message to the known addressee. In small villages the anonymity of the cities is just not possible, so each one is acquainted with the others. Even if the addressee happens not to be known, the letter-sender is reckoned as a friend and because of this both old and young want to send suitable messages.

If someone knows the uncle especially well, he is eager to preach to the nephew about duty; if another is intimate with the nephew he desires to send respectful salutations to the maternal uncle. If one woman is known to the maternal aunt, she wishes to send good wishes to the husband of the cousin. Being a friend of the niece, it becomes necessary to send respectful greetings to the father-in-law of the aunt. Under these conditions, the difference between relationship and lack of it, between acquaintance and lack of it, has hardly any significance.

And it would be unseemly for anyone to waste the chance to have something written by a person like me. Instead of a greasy envelope from the shopkeeper's shelf, an envelope with the whiteness of a duck's feathers comes out of my bag. Compared with the use of the wrapper from spices, the pages of my notebook appear neater and bigger. The lidless inkpot and black reed pen in the courtyard of the village revenue record-keeper obviously do not have the attraction of my shiny fountain pen. Compared with the dirty, crumpled stamps brought tied in the folds of someone's loincloth, my stamps appear more reliable. One who does not get a letter written by a person having such superior letter-writing implements is obviously exposing his naiveté about worldly behaviour. That is why all request me to write at least two words on their behalf.

Never once has the question been raised by them as to why it is necessary for me to discharge the difficult functions of the Post Office, or whether letters written by me will reach the addressee or not, whether my stamps and envelopes are really reliable or whether or not my letter writing was proof of my being useless.

Even if a person goes to the city imbued with the highest ideals of service, he becomes a victim of the shafts of doubt and disbelief. Society's habit of doubting without any reason petrifies his determination to serve and its aimless dissimulation stultifies his life philosophy. Against this, the book of the villager's life is invariably open. Certain adverse circumstances may generate exceptions, but where life is somewhat healthier, a villager's offer of help is rendered naturally, without humiliating the other. Assistance is offered as matter of course, without arrogance, and the exchange of ideas, being without artificiality, supplements the study of life.

One day, seeing me writing something, an old woman came over to me to get a letter written to her son who lived in some distant city. Others then followed and ultimately letter writing for others became my duty. I myself, even if there is need to write a letter, hardly send any, and there is no question of writing letters for no reason. Therefore despite making arrangements for stamps, envelopes and postcards, this professional letter writing has not proved to be expensive.

I have many places to sit for letter writing. Sometimes, resting my back against the trunk of the peepal tree, I use its raised roots as my throne, or I sit beneath the mango tree on a sheet of dried leaves. Sometimes I will sit on a narrow bed on someone's verandah or in someone's courtyard on a mat in front of the mud platform on which the holy tulsi plant grows. Whoever it is who makes the first request for a letter, others have to follow his wishes. The person dictating the letter sits near me, the others a little apart near one another. Persons who only wish to send greetings drift in and out.

One person, entrusting the drawing of water for irrigation to one of his friends, rushes to get his salutation inscribed. Reminding me to send his benediction, someone else goes away to winnow. To get her message written, a woman tarries for a while with a water vessel perched on her head and the rope used to draw water held in her hands. One remembers that she has to grind gram as soon as she has had her greetings written, and another, giving a piece of thick chappati to a crying child, rushes in to hear the end of the letter. While speaking sermon-like sentences, someone gets up to rekindle his hubble-bubble before it goes out.

Such wanderings to and fro keep occurring. It is only the letter writer, sometimes laughing, sometimes crying and sometimes seated sadly, who has to take care of the story from the beginning to the end. After the letter is finished, he has to read out the full contents aloud. Not only this, but he has to add a line here and a line there to the subject matter according to the wishes of the sender. Then the sender becomes eager to authenticate the letter as his own by applying his thumb impression. Although such an action might protect a person against the untruths prevalent in the world, in the self-expressed feelings conveyed in a letter it has no value, but not many are willing to accept this fact. That is why, below the names, picturesque impressions of variously shaped thumbs often smudge the letters.

The inscription of the address is the most difficult aspect of this letter writing. Someone is called Nanhku though his real name is Mahabir. Someone is called Dularua, 'Adorable One', at home and outside he is known as Bhairodin, a fierce god. Someone is called Ghasita, 'Dragged One', in his village but in other villages is called Raja Ram, 'King Ram'. One woman will be called Sirtajia, 'Royal One', in her maternal grandfather's home, and Dukhia, 'Unhappy One', at her father's house. The family members may call some woman Rupmatia, 'Beautiful', while others call her Kaluia, 'Ugly Dark One'.

It need not surprise us if the conjunctions of a person's name and nickname, despite their contrary meanings, remind one of the poets. Here a person, although poor and dark as coal, may be called Hiralal, 'Diamond', and bear the nickname of Shardendu, 'Moon Rays', but not be considered a laughing stock. Poverty is contingent on the social structure, appearance is a gift of nature, and a name would be considered a gift from one's parents. The only thing left is the nickname, for which the person is fully responsible. Possibly because of this, disregarding the absence of the quality in question, or not worrying about the quality, they like to possess the names given by the world to very beautiful things.

The pseudonyms for which poets have traditionally shown partiality naturally attract the attention of pseudonym hunters, but it seems peculiar if there is no similarity between the name and the person to whom it refers. Since the audience might forget the relationship between the name and the pseudonym, these poets always present both names together.

But the system of giving names and nicknames in villages is entirely different. The name is given by the priest on the basis of his religious books, but the nickname gives the real picture of either the person's looks, nature, qualities or what others think of him.

If someone is called 'Babbler', he will not be entirely devoid of this quality. If one is called 'Petite cowherd-woman', she will invariably be dressed like a doll in coloured dresses. If someone is caled 'Nightingale', she is bound to be dark and soft-spoken. The one who is called 'Pierced Nose' must have had to wear a nose ring after his birth. If a man is called 'Rubbish', he must have suffered great neglect as a child. There may be exceptions in a few cases, but generally the meaning coincides with the attributes of the person and is not contrary.

But when writing a letter it becomes difficult to know which of the two names the person in the distant place would choose to be given prominence. As long as he is in familiar surroundings, persons familiar with his qualities choose an appropriate name for him. But when the person has to introduce himself, then which of the two names given to him will be acceptable to him depends on his own inclinations and his feelings toward others. In this respect the person dictating and the writer both grope in darkness.

After one has solved the mystery of the name, the difficulty of getting an address raises its head. Generally, except for the name of the city, nothing else is known to them. One may not be mystified but will definitely be surprised when observing their belief in the fame of the recipient. A man will firmly believe that everyone must be familiar with the appearance of his beloved son. Another is convinced that the whole city will know the name of his wrestler nephew. Yet another believes that the fame of a singer must have reached the Post Office. One believes that the postman could not be unacquainted with his uncle who cures snake and scorpion bites by faith healing. A woman will suppose that the fame of her husband as an amateur veterinary doctor is a sufficient address. Someone will say that the learnedness of his maternal uncle, who has memorized the whole prayerbook to Hanuman, could not remain circumscribed.

They are unwilling either to know or accept that their near and dear ones are like drops in the ocean in a big city.

After identifying the address through these mazes and completing the letter, it becomes necessary to take it to the Post Office immediately. One, sticking the letter in his headgear or in his jacket and taking a tumbler and rope to draw water from well on the road in case he gets thirsty, starts at once for the Post Office three miles away. Another, in order to take the letter in the morning, gets his luggage ready the evening before. One will tuck the letter in a reed box for safety while he finishes his work. And someone else, affectionately caressing the letter with his fingers, will smudge the ink.

Many a time I have to drop the letter in the Post Office myself, but they prefer to post the letters themselves, and in this respect have less faith in me. They are confident that they will not make a mistake in recognizing the red mailbox, but they are not sure that the person to whom I might entrust this job will not make a mistake. The great number of mailboxes and water taps found in the city does not allow them to be confident about the ability of someone else who might be entrusted with this job to recognize the genuine mailbox.

The days spent waiting for the reply keep them even busier. The village is visited by the postman only once a week, but the letter senders will generally run to the Post Office themselves almost every day. Hearing the reply that no letter is there for them will not, however, satisfy them. Repeating name and nickname, they ask that the mail be checked again and thereby get rebuked by the postal clerk. Someone, in the hope of getting his letter traced, will repeatedly narrate his ancestry and the name of the village, thus annoying even the postman.

Even I keep my patience with difficulty when answering queries about the replies which are expected to come to my address.

Someone will ask how many days it will take to get a reply. Someone will ask whether I am sure that the address was correctly written. Another will ponder aloud within my hearing that the attributes of the addressee were not written along with his name, so the letter cannot have reached him. Someone will raise the doubt that since the stamp was old the postal clerk may have thrown the letter into the wastebasket. Someone else is apprehensive as to whether, due to the rains, the address might have been washed away. Another will be convinced that since the letter was heavy and had insufficient postage it might be shuttling aimlessly about unclaimed.

Sometimes I just laugh and on other occasions get angry at their ignorance. Sometimes I feel irritated, and sometimes repentant because of their helplessness. Who has rendered these people, who are so eager to exchange ideas and sentiments, so utterly helpless? Those who keep such a large population incommunicado and are proud of their own hairsplitting – how shameless they are! Such questions are bound to be asked.

Despite all these problems, the letter writing has been managed somehow, but one day when a mute woman caught hold of the edge of my sari in supplication and began making varied gestures requesting a letter to be written, I was really thunderstruck. Was there no end to my pitiable condition? Would I have to write letters for a mute? To whom did she want to send a letter? How would I ever know?

But the person regarding whom these problems had arisen appeared not at all concerned about their resolution. Perhaps, having observed me writing so many letters, she had forgotten her pathetic incapacity. It was not easy for that mute woman to believe that after writing so many sad and happy stories a person would not also be able to understand her obvious sadness or happiness.

Having seen her many times, I was now used to her presence. Whenever I reached the village I would find her waiting for me. When I left she would escort me for quite a long distance, walking behind me. Whenever I was writing she would squat near me and watch my activities with curiosity. But so far I had assumed she was merely a curious visitor, and I was taken aback when she herself wished to send a letter.

She is called 'Gungia' because of her muteness. Her real name is Dhanpatia, 'Rich One'. Her father Raghu was a prosperous and honest oil-extractor. A pair of strong bullocks belonged to the household, and the oil-extractor used to grind everything from mustard seed to castor-oil seeds. The purity of his oil and the good quality of his oil cakes were known even beyond his village.

She was the first child of her parents and her birth was celebrated with unusual aplomb. The drum beaters came asking for their gifts, a low-caste woman danced in her honour and took away a fine sari in exchange, and several drums full of ghee were consumed by the feasting fellow caste-men.

The mother was given a compote prepared from dry fruits and spices, and a mixture of flour, sugar and the gum of the babul tree. When, after five weeks had passed, the mother emerged from the delivery room with the child in her arms, many rituals were observed in order to ward off the evil eye and to protect the health of both of them. So much unguent was applied to the body of the child that her hairless body became as smooth as dough made of white flour. So much oil was applied that one could not steadily gaze on the glare of her shiny skin.

Roly-poly Dhanpatia began walking even before she was ten months old, but she did not speak even after reaching her fifth year. She could say neither 'mama' nor 'papa'; neither 'milk' nor even 'goo-goo'. She could only express her wishes by crying 'wah! wah!' in different pitches.

When she passed the age when most children begin talking, her parents became anxious. Amulets and threads blessed by priests were tied around her wrists. The assistance of magic incantations was invoked and also treatment by faith healers. Vows, worship, religious performances, all were tried but Dhanpatia remained mute. In the end Raghu took her to a doctor in the city. The deformity in her palate could only be removed by surgery and he had neither the money nor the courage for such a venture. As a result, Dhanpatia grew up as a mute. But by not bestowing deafness also on her, God had made her handicap more galling. In the absence of hearing, muteness is not so painful as when it is accompanied by it. After Dhanpatia, one more daughter was born to the family and she was not mute.

Dhanpatia as if to compensate for her lack of speech, grew very sensitive. She was so clever that whatever she saw done even once she would never forget and every activity she learned she could repeat without any mistakes. Reaching the age of eight or nine years, she began assisting her mother in all her duties.

Now it became necessary to resolve the problem of marriage. To avoid the stigma of spinsterhood, Raghu adopted the usual ruse of parents of girls unsaleable on the marriage market. Having got his pre-pubescent daughter engaged in some distant village, he completed the formalities of the marriage while she sat underneath the marriage canopy. When she went to her in-laws' place after three or four years for consummation, she became aware of her pitiable condition. She did not talk and when, on being compelled, she began crying 'wah, wah', her husband's family went wild with rage at being cheated.

'She is mute. Her father has defrauded us. Snatch away her jewellery and throw her out.'

Hearing these words, for the first time she glimpsed the tragedy of her deformity, which had been covered up at her parents' place by their affection.

With utter humility she caught hold of the feet of her mother-in-law and despite being kicked she continued crying, hiding her face, but no one took pity on her. Cheating is cheating. If the person who perpetrated the fraud cannot be punished, his progeny has to suffer. Otherwise where would the majesty of justice be? In the end, they stopped only after they had taken away all her jewellery and clothes, and despatched her to her parents' house.

As it was, Raghu was uncomfortable at his action. As recompense for the injustice, he sent a proposal that his second daughter be married to the same bridegroom, and thus peace was restored. This time the bride was subjected to proper scrutiny and on an auspicious day the marriage was solemnized. The old women of the village still talk about how, on seeing her sister marry her own husband, decked in her marriage ornaments and clothes, Gungia, the mute one, could control her sobbing only by stuffing her mouth with the edge of her sari.

After her sister left, she tried to assuage the suffering of her parents by silently serving them.

Since then, time had not stood still and her parents and in-laws had returned to the dust. Her sister had given birth to two children but neither lived beyond three years. Perhaps unable to bear the thought of her third child's premature death, she left it motherless. Not able to make arrangements for the child's upbringing, the father brought him to his in-laws' place and, putting the baby in the mute one's arms, started crying.

In the blinking eyes of the baby, mute like herself, what message she read Gungia alone knows, but she could not return the child. In a hushed voice the brother-in-law proposed that she come to his village, but he did not pursue the subject when he saw the determined expression of refusal on her face.

The villagers were surprised at the child-rearing of the mute mother. She sold one bullock and bought two goats to give the baby milk; she made a cap and jacket from her expensive brocade sari for the baby; melting her arm bracelet she made bangles, a waist band and other jewellery for the child, and on the day he was formally given a name she feasted the whole village, spending her hoarded money.

After the death of her parents her trade had already shrunk, and now she was kept busy looking after the child. In this way, as Hulasi started growing, Gungia's wealth started shrinking. At first the father did enquire about his son but later, due to love for his new wife and child, he forgot him, and the mute one never asked anything from him nor reduced the expensive upbringing of the child.

For some time, since she and her son were both mute, they understood each other's thoughts through gestures. As he began talking, however, he was mystified by his mother's lack of speech and when he grew to an understanding age he became ashamed of his mother's muteness. When boys of the village teased him, calling 'Mute's son, mute's son', he felt heartbroken. He would sometimes go out to beat them and sometimes would just sit there crying. When, hearing the noise, the mute woman would come out and begin reprimanding them with her 'wah, wah' accompanied by a variety of gestures, shouting 'Mute auntie, mute auntie', the naughty boys would melt away.

Taking Hulasi inside, she would make the child sit in her lap, give him sweets from an earthen pot, comb the dirt from his hair with her fingers, wipe his face with the edge of her sari, and through various gestures try to explain to the child. But this treatment only increased his discomfiture. Pushing his mother aside with both his tiny hands, he would sprawl face down in the mud courtyard and begin crying still more loudly, or sometimes, tugging the edge of his mother's sari, would pleadingly ask, 'Everyone else's mother talks – why are you the only mute one?' What answer could she, the mute one, give to this question? In her motherly love and care she was second to none, but what could she do about her muteness?

As Hulasi grew, he came to know some false and some true stories about his life from the lips of others. Gungia could not speak and so many false stories remained uncontradicted such as that she, being annoyed with her sister for snatching away her home and husband, had taken revenge by kidnapping the son from his father. The love which she showed to Hulasi definitely had some evil motive. Even though he did not fully understand the import of such hints, still his heart began veering away from his mute foster-mother.

There is an abundance of covetous people whose mouths, in the words of the saint poet Tulsidas, 'water at some else's butter', and thanks to them even the niggardly happiness of Gungia had to give way to a spasm of pain. There was no one to tell him of the helpless condition in which he was left to her care by his father, how much neglect the father had shown in his upbringing and how hard the new wife had tried to keep Hulasi away from his father in order to protect the interest of her own children.

The depth of Gungia's silent love was beyond his reach. Besides, receiving abundant love from her, he took it as his right instead of as a gift from someone who was not his mother.

One day Hulasi asked her why she had taken him away from his father. The words pierced her heart like a poisoned arrow and she broke down but could not give expression to her grief. Her mouth, unable to form words, stayed open, her eyes dimmed with surprise and her facial expression froze in sadness. These signs, however, remained a riddle for the child.

She launched a search for his father and information came that, finding some job in a factory, he had settled down in the industrial town of Kanpur with his family. Thereupon, pawning her bangles, she made arrangements to send Hulasi to his father. New clothes were sewn for Hulasi. Coloured wooden and clay toys were arranged neatly in a reed box. Fried mahua, jaggery and sweets were tied in a bundle. A smoke-blackened, smooth earthen pot was filled with ghee.

She begged a wise man who was treated as an uncle by her to escort Hulasi to his father. Then one day, at a particular time declared auspicious by the village priest, withholding her tears lest she bring bad luck, she walked three miles to the railway station to bid farewell to Hulasi and her uncle. As the train steamed away she found it difficult even to get back to her village. She sometimes stood on the mounds between two fields, sometimes sat beneath shady trees, sometimes laughed, sometimes cried, and thus she reached her home and until dawn lay sprawled in the courtyard with her face propped on the tiny mud platform of the holy tulsi plant.

For several days she remained sad and downcast. Then one day she decided to begin working and as she opened the door of the house her eyes espied the mud-splattered uncle and Hulasi behind him, walking towards her. The child's new clothes had become dirty and his face had grown ashen. She ran and embraced the son and in wordless, indistinct crying expressed her sorrow at their parting.

Later the result of the trip became known. After wandering for two days they had met Hulasi's father. He lived in a narrow, dirty lane, having rented two dark airless rooms, with his wife and her four children. The affection which lit up his eyes on seeing his long-forgotten son was later lost under the hard gaze of his new wife. The husband and wife quarrelled the whole night through.

In the morning, giving many reasons, the father asked the uncle to take Hulasi back to the village. Whatever property was at Hulasi's maternal grandparents' place belonged to Hulasi, but his father was the only provider for his four other children. Whether Hulasi lived with his father's new family or with mute Gungia, he would not be with his real mother; therefore he should stay at his grandparents' place and take care of the trade, house, fields and cash which were his due there. When his step-brother grew up he would also be sent to him. His father's present wife was eager to go and live in the village, and although this would not be acceptable to mute Gungia, she was not immortal, and after her death they would all go and take over the family's property in the village.

Neither the tears of Hulasi nor the entreaties of the uncle proved of any avail against this utilitarian approach. Helpless, like defeated soldiers, both returned crestfallen. The wife, acting as if they were gifts sent to her, kept the pot filled with ghee, the sweets, toys and new clothes meant for Hulasi, and distributed them to her children.

In this way Hulasi returned to Gungia bereft of any belongings. The poor mother then tried her best to assuage the hurt feelings of the child with her affection. In addition, she began working very hard to buy his beloved toys and clothes again, but it was difficult to heal his broken faith. Man is always pining for whatever is unattainable, and accordingly Hulasi was heartsick for his father, brothers and sisters. The reason his father had not kept him was Gungia's money and property, and they would be able to live together once she was gone – these thoughts began poisoning his mind.

In this way two more years went by. By then, feeling somewhat recompensed, Hulasi began sharing Gungia's work. But due to destiny's prank, a holy man with several disciples came to the village. They had arrived at the village in the course of their wanderings, but with the onset of the rainy season they decided to pass the next four months camping in the mango grove of the village landlord.

The arrival of such a holy man was taken as a great event by the villagers. One offered a bucketful of milk and someone else gave a pitcher of ghee. Another offered a ripe pumpkin as a gift and someone else a lump of jaggery. Someone would leave fine aged rice for him and someone else milled white flour. Another wanted to give him a feast of malpua, and someone else wished to give fried wheat-cakes and rice pudding.

These offers were not made without underlying motives. All these devout people wanted at least one boon from the holy man. One was eager for a son in his old age. Another needed money. One wanted somebody to lose a court case. Someone else desired magic incantations in order to persuade his brother to renounce all worldly possessions. One wanted an incantation to draw his beloved to him. Another wanted to know how to redeem his mortgaged fields without paying the money which was due. In order to snatch back his pawned jewellery, someone wished that the mind of the creditor be confused. One wanted to be cured without taking any medicines. In brief, almost all these devotees would sit with hands folded in supplication before the holy man, hiding either proper or improper desires in their hearts.

It seemed as if the holy man had appeared as a personification of the saying, 'He came meaning to pray, but instead he spun cotton.' Applying a paste of ash on his body, black like a lump of smoking tobacco, placing a wig on his head and holding up a sceptre of steel tongs, he conducted the court of these devotees while seated on a reed mat. His way of offering boons was no less strange. Toward one devotee he would merely glance with a beaming countenance, toward another he would gesture with his hand to be patient, the rattling of his tongs would express his dissatisfaction with another, an offering of ash from the holy fire would satisfy someone else; in this way no one went away from him either fully gratified or totally disappointed.

If one of the villagers felt that the holy man was somewhat less inclined to grant his request, he would begin serving him with greater zeal, and one to whom he was especially kind would bring more offerings to make the benevolence permanent.

Naturally he was especially solicitous toward women devotees. If some village bride narrated the tale of neglect by her husband or a sad story of childlessness, his eyes, red from smoking marijuana, would shine with greater lust.

Three or four adolescent disciples would busy themselves day and night serving the holy man. One of them would wear only a strip of cloth covering his private parts, and another would walk about wrapped in only a scarf. One had his head shaved; the other had difficulty keeping his wig in position. One, while bringing food given as an offering to the holy man, would taste a morsel, and the other would take a puff of the marijuana pipe while lighting it. The curious boys of the village would hang around the holy man and Hulasi too began visiting the camp along with them.

The holy man had a knack of divining a great deal by observing facial expressions and behaviour, and by overhearing conversations. How far he already had knowledge of Hulasi is difficult to say, but one day, pretending to notice Hulasi for the first time, he spoke in this way: 'Ah! You are destined to become a great yogi, boy; your forehead has real lustre, but in your heart – come near me, boy, and let me read your fate lines.'

Like the breath of a python which draws the selected prey towards its mouth, the eyes of the holy man pulled the boy near him. After that day Hulasi was unable to overcome his mysterious attraction.

Mute Gungia also had sent him an offering of sesame, jaggery, oil and other articles, but she had neither the voice nor desire to ask any boon. But when Hulasi began hovering there day and night she grew anxious. One day, right under the nose of the holy man, holding Hulasi's hand she dragged him away. But the next day, disregarding her wishes, he went to the camp again. Finding no way out, spreading the edge of her sari before him in supplication, she begged the holy man to leave her only son in peace.

The holy man may have felt some pity, or perhaps merely in mockery he told Hulasi to go home and not to return to the camp. After that Hulasi was never seen there. A few days before the rainy season was going to be over, the villagers found the mango grove empty one morning. The holy man had apparently left the place during the night. Hearing the news of his disappearance and observing Hulasi's empty bed, Gungia beat her breast. Not finding him anywhere in the village, she ran for several miles crying bitterly, but there was no trace of the holy man. A few days later information came that a similar group had been seen that very night boarding a train at the railway station four or five miles way. No other information could be obtained.

Gungia's tragedy became a source of amusement for the villagers. One would tease her, 'The holy man has come, Gungia.' Someone else would say in jest, 'A telegram has come from Hulasi.' Another would taunt, 'What did you expect to come of it when you pretended to be a mother and adopted another's child?'

But Gungia neither understood nor knew anything except that she was waiting for Hulasi. She would search for one knew not what among the children of the village. Seeing a new toy she would immediately buy it and lock it safely in her reed box. Seeing a new piece of cloth, she would have a shirt sewn in Hulasi's size, and folding it neatly would lock it in her wooden box. She would buy sweets that Hulasi used to like and keep them in the hanging pouch. Sometimes, in the silence of the night, opening the door of the house she would wait for the sound of footsteps. She had complete faith that one day Hulasi would return to her, but he never came.

When I saw Gungia for the first time, twelve or thirteen years had already passed. Except for his mute mother everyone else had forgotten Hulasi.

Suddenly, several years later, a man who had returned to the village gave information that Hulasi had become a watchman at the residence of some millionaire in Calcutta, and that he was now married and had several children. To what extent there was an element of truth in this story only the narrator knew, but even in this gossip the villagers found an excuse to tease Gungia.

Since Hulasi had now become a rich man he would come to show Gungia round the city and drive her in a car. Thus they mocked her, but for Gungia even this jest was truth.

Instead of resenting the son who, after running away, had not even bothered to enquire about her, she grew more affectionate. She mused over the difficulties under which her son must have passed his days. Who would have cooked his meals and looked after his clothes in that foreign territory? The holy man must have bewitched her son, and then when he came to himself and remembered his home there must have been no money to return to the village. Now, having had a run of good luck, he had become a decent householder. How could he know that his mute mother was still alive? He must feel shy about writing to someone else in the village and the thought that no one would remember him after so many years must have prevented him from writing. But, nevertheless, he should write to his mute mother. He would run to her the moment he heard from her. The daughter-in-law would also come. Wouldn't the grandchildren demand to see their own grandmother? Musing over these things, one day Gungia decided to get a letter written on her behalf.

But this was not easily done. After writing 'To the most prosperous and incomparable Hulasi, oil-extractor, his mother Gungia sends her blessings,' the pen stopped. When I asked her, 'Should I write that it was wrong of you to have run away?', waving her hand she asked me not to do so. 'What you did was very good?' – When I asked if I should write this, she again shook her head. When I asked if I should write 'Your mother Gungia has waited for you for the past twelve years,' she nodded agreement. Writing in this manner, like a novice poet constructing and reconstructing verses, I somehow completed the letter.

No one knew his address; therefore, writing on the envelope 'To Hulasi Din, Oil-extractor, Calcutta', I took leave of Gungia. She herself posted the letter. But I could not shake off my responsibility merely by writing this letter, for whenever Gungia found me she would harry me and ask questions through her gestures about the fate of her letter, which was probably languishing somewhere in a dead letter office.

One of my classmates was undergoing treatment by a doctor in Calcutta and after telling her the story of Gungia I requested that

she somehow locate Hulasi. After a week, the reply which I received
from her was filled with abuse. To imagine that, without any
address, she would be able to locate an insignificant person like
Hulasi in the midst of this seething mass of humanity was only
indicative of my utter stupidity. Such a person as I, devoid
of any knowledge about practicability, would be better off not
meddling with the problems of others. Receiving this sermon
instead of Hulasi's address, it was understandable that I felt
irritated.

More days thus went by. In the meantime Gungia fell ill. For
many months she had suffered from a fever which finally revealed
itself as tuberculosis. But she stopped working only when she
could not get up from bed any more. As bouts of coughing
increased, the number of visitors declined. A distant relative of
hers was taking care of her oil-machine and bullocks and his
daughter did some nursing of the sick woman.

Whenever I went to visit the ailing Gungia, disregarding her
fatigue she would ask through varied gestures about the letter
from Hulasi.

In the meantime my classmate had written to me again.
She informed me that her new servant, Har Bhajan, was entrusted
with the job of locating Hulasi and although he had not so far
been able to find him, he was very unhappy after hearing the story
of Gungia. His village was located somewhere nearby and he had
run away about ten or twelve years back without telling his
mother. His mother was now dead, but it was his firm belief
that by giving a little happiness to Gungia he would please his
mother's soul. Proud of having been in school up to the third
grade, he was himself writing a disjointed letter to Gungia. He
also wanted to send some money to Gungia. He would not
accept having his mistress send money on his behalf, but wanted
to send money earned by the sweat of his brow. He hoped
that in my love of truthfulness I would not destroy the little
satisfaction which he was trying to give to that dying mother.

A week later, Har Bhajan's letter and a money order for ten
rupees reached the village. News had come from Calcutta; hearing
this, Gungia assumed the letter-writer to be Hulasi. Therefore
it was not necessary to tell her the truth or to speak lies. From
Har Bhajan's letter, also, no one could say for sure who had

written and to whom, for all that a village son could write to his
mother was inscribed there.

> Mother, even if I served you for many lives I would not be able
> to repay my debt to you. For me you are my god. My mind
> was mad, otherwise why would I have left a mother like you
> in order to wander in the world? Now I will return to your
> holy feet again. There is a delay only because I am not able to
> get time off. Do not worry about anything. Your benediction
> hovers over my head like an umbrella. I will never be in
> trouble. Your daughter-in-law and grandson send their respects.

Holding that dirty and torn piece of paper in her emaciated,
skeleton-like fingers and pressing it to her perforated bosom, she
closed her eyes; but through the corners of her wrinkled eyelids a
thin stream of tears trickled down, touching her ears, and fell on
the dirty, greasy pillow.

One month after this she was found dead amidst the open reed
box of Hulasi's toys and the wooden box of clothes. The ten
rupee note was found untouched beneath her pillow.

I tried to find out more about Har Bhajan, but he never came to
the area with his common-law wife, and trying to locate him in
the big city after he had left my classmate's service would have
been as difficult as finding Hulasi.

The strange persons I have seen and the unbelievable stories I
have heard concerning them in my lifetime far outshine any creations
of the imagination. But the sense of pathos and mystery that
gripped my heart when I observed Gungia's life never rose again.

My letter-writing still continues. At that time I used to write
letters containing the life stories of others for my amusement; now
I watch the sadness and happiness of others' lives in search
of another character like Gungia. But in the world there are more
concentricities of ignorance than of knowledge, and it is not
easy for the moments which give insights into life's mysteries
to repeat themselves.

Sometimes I wonder whether the image of that silent, vibrant
motherly affection will alone remain in my memory.

Glossary

Alaknanda: the name of the river Ganges as it flows through the Himalayas.

Allahabad: the modern name of the ancient city of Prayag situated at the confluence of the two holy rivers, the Ganges and the Yamuna, and the mythical, invisible river Saraswati. Pilgrims flock to the city for ritual bathing in the rivers and every twelfth year a major fair is held. The city is located in Northern India in the state of Uttar Pradesh.

Allha Udal epic: a bardic composition depicting the heroic deeds and travails of two brothers, Allha and Udal. It is sung in villages during the rainy season.

babul tree: a thorny bush which normally grows wild.

Badrinath: a temple located at a height of 10,000 feet above sea level in the central Himalayas. One of the four temples which a devout Hindu is expected to visit before his death.

Basant Panchmi Day: an auspicious day for ritual bathing in the holy rivers.

Brahmin: the highest caste among Hindus.

chappati: whole wheat dough rolled into a thin, round form and baked either entirely on a hot, ungreased griddle or sometimes partly on the griddle and partly direct on the fuel source. Chappatis are one of the main items of food in the meals of North Indians and Pakistanis.

Chitra Gupta: Considered to be God's record keeper, he maintains an account of all the sinful and pious deeds of mortals and presents the facts to God after the human's death, on which basis heaven or hell is allotted.

chutney: a sauce made of ground tamarind, hot chillies, mint, coriander and one or more of many other vegetables or fruits, including unripe mangoes.

coolie: a labourer of any sort, denoting lack of skill and low wages.

dandi: a wooden palanquin in which the rider is carried on the shoulders of two coolies.

dhamri: a coin of small value, now no longer in use. Two dhamri were equal to one paise, with sixty-four paise in a rupee.

Dharamraj: the keeper of heaven, responsible to God.

Dotiyal: a tribe living in the central Himalayas, known for their hardiness and simplicity.

Ganesh: a God whose head is that of an elephant, and body that of a man. He is felt to bring prosperity and is worshipped first in any religious ceremony.

ghee: butter which has been clarified by slow cooking. It is used as a cooking medium.

gram: a term used for various kinds of leguminous vegetables like chick peas, horse gram, mung beans, etc.

gur: same as *jaggery,* below.

halvah: a pulpy fried mixture, generally of whole wheat flour cooked in clarified butter and mixed with sugar and water. Generally served as a dessert.

Hanuman: the powerful god who has the form of a monkey. In the epic *Ram Charit Manas* he fought against the forces of evil and is considered a perfect celibate, invincible, immortal and the greatest devotee of Lord Ram. He is widely worshipped in Northern India.

Harish Chandra: a king of Northern India, mentioned in the *Puranas,* who was famous for his charities and his truthfulness. He gave away all his possessions as gifts and was then forced to become a serf in Benares in order to earn a living. In Indian folklore his name is synonymous with absolute truthfulness.

Holi: a festival of revelry in Northern India during which people throw coloured water at each other.

jaggery: unpurified sugar or molasses.

Kabir: a famous saint and poet living in the sixteenth century in the city of Benares.

Kalyug: Hindus divide time into four main ages – Satyug, Treta,

Dwaper and Kalyug, each of 3,456,000, 1,728,000, 864,000 and 432,000 solar years respectively. Satyug was the age of perfection and divinity which slowly degenerated into the modern age of Kalyug. Kalyug is the period when non-ethical forces rise and untruth triumphs, and people lose their moral standards. Kalyug is thus synonymous with immorality and falsehood.

karhi: ground and fried mixture of gram and peas dipped in a curry sauce of buttermilk and gram flour.

Kedarnath: a temple in the central Himalayas located near the temple of Badrinath.

kichri: a boiled mixture of rice and lentils with condiments and salt.

Krishna: the main character in the epic *Mahabarat*, considered an incarnation of God and worshipped throughout India.

Kumbh Fair: Every twelfth year the Magh Fair (see below) held at Allahabad becomes the Kumbh Fair. It is one of the major festivals for religious immersion in India.

kurta: a loose, almost knee-length shirt made of cotton or wool and generally worn by men.

Kut-pad: a type of poetry in which the mystical or religious meaning is not immediately apparent and has to be indirectly inferred from the words.

Lakshmi: the consort of Lord Vishnu, the main God of the Hindu trinity consisting of Vishnu, Brahma and Shiva. Lakshmi is the goddess of wealth and prosperity.

Magh Fair: a bathing festival held every year in the city of Allahabad at the confluence of the two holy rivers, the Ganges and the Yamuna.

mahua: the flower of a tree of the same name which can be used for sweetening any preparation including sweet cakes of wheat flour. It is also used in distilling a particular type of liquor.

malpua: a sweet pancake.

Mem Sahib: a term originally used during British rule to refer to the wives of English functionaries. Now in general use for the wife of any man of high status.

neem tree: a large, shady tree whose twigs are used to clean teeth.

paise: a subdivision of the rupee. Currently there are 100 paise to a rupee. At the time this book was written in Hindi, there were 64 paise to a rupee, a rupee then being approximately one fifth of an American dollar, or one shilling.

panchamrit: a decoction of yoghurt, water, raisins, sugar, milk and condiments, which is offered to the Gods and is afterward distributed to the devotees.

peepal tree: a large leafy tree, considered holy.

pua: a small piece of sweetened whole wheat dough which is fried in oil or clarified butter and stuffed with raisins.

puri: a thin round of whole wheat dough which puffs up in the process of deep frying. Eaten with vegetables or meat throughout India and served especially on festive occasions.

Rama: the main character in the epic *Ram Charit Manas,* commonly known as the *Ramayana* epic. He is considered to have been a reincarnation of God who was sent to eradicate the evil and demons who had become too powerful and overbearing. He is widely worshipped by Hindus throughout India.

Ramayana: the story of the life and adventures of Ram and his consort Sita.

Rewa: an old state under the British Paramountcy, now part of the new state of Madhya Pradesh. Its main city is also called Rewa.

rupee: the basic Indian monetary unit. At the present official rates, $7\frac{1}{2}$ rupees are equivalent to one American dollar and £1.00 equals 18 rupees. (See note for *paise.*)

Sankranti: one of the most auspicious days for bathing in the river Ganges.

sattu: a quick Indian snack made of ground barley and gram flour, eaten after adding water and salt or jaggery.

Shaligram: an idol of Lord Shiva.

Shastra: ancient and holy scriptures of the Hindus.

Shiva: one member of the Hindu trinity of Brahma, Vishnu and Shiva. He is known as the Destroyer and is symbolized in temples by a stone phallus in a vagina. He is considered very beneficent and the perfect Yogi. Worshipped throughout India.

Sita: the consort of Ram in the *Ramayana* epic. She is considered very virtuous and was the incarnation of Lakshmi, the goddess of wealth.

tonga: a high, two-wheeled cart drawn by a horse.

tulsi: the basil plant. Considered holy and auspicious, its leaves are offered to the gods and then distributed to the devotees. The plant is found in every temple and in most homes in an Indian village. Made into tea, its leaves are considered to have medicinal value.

Tulsidas: a famous saint and poet of the seventeenth century who was the author of the epic *Ramayana* which is still much read throughout Northern India and studied for its moral and spiritual values.

Ulat basia: a type of poetry in which the meaning can only be discerned by inverting the sequence of the lines.

vermilion: a bright red pigment, mercuric sulphide, placed on the forehead in the centre parting of the hair by married Hindu women whose husbands are alive.

Yamuna: one of the holy rivers of the Hindus.